Feed Me!
I'm Yours

By Vicki Lansky

Illustrations by Pat Seitz

BANTAM BOOKS

NEW YORK • TORONTO • LONDON • SYDNEY • AUCKLAND

This book was written in 1974 by six mothers, all members of the Childbirth Education Association (CEA) of Minneapolis/ St. Paul. CEA is a non-profit organization that prepares couples for a rewarding childbirth experience.

This edition contains the complete text of the original hardcover edition.
NOT ONE WORD HAS BEEN OMITTED.

FEED ME! I'M YOURS
A Bantam Book/published by arrangement with Meadowbrook Press, Inc.

PRINTING HISTORY

Meadowbrook edition published October 1974
Bantam edition/February 1977
Updated Bantam edition/March 1979
Updated Bantam edition/March 1989

ISBN 0-553-27251-9

Published simultaneously in the United States and Canada

Bantam Books are published by Bantam Books, a division of Bantam Doubleday Dell Publishing Group, Inc. Its trademark, consisting of the words "Bantam Books" and the portrayal of a rooster, is Registered in U.S. Patent and Trademark Office and in other countries. Marca Registrada. Bantam Books, 666 Fifth Avenue, New York, New York 10103.

PRINTED IN THE UNITED STATES OF AMERICA
RAD   33   32   31   30   29   28   27   26

Dedication

To Parents Everywhere
from those of us who have been there
and
wish we knew then what we know now

In the beginning, you'll be choosing between breastfeeding (the original health food) and formula, but at least these are two sides of the same coin—enriched milk. The field of food choices widens significantly by the time your child is six months old and for the next number of years the responsibility for your child's food selection is mainly yours.

With this recipe book, we have tried to help you with that selection. Our recipes and ideas have been collected for their nutrition, convenience and fun. We hope this effort will ease your task of meal preparation and help you enjoy your young infant, toddler or pre-schooler while he or she is keeping you company at home.

Vicki Lansky and
Jill Jacobson
Stephanie Keane
Norine Larson
Mary Popehn
Lois Parker

ABOUT THE AUTHORS

In April of 1974 six members of the Childbirth Education Association of Minneapolis-St. Paul got together to write a cookbook. They felt that CEA and other groups were doing a good job of helping women through childbirth, but there was a dearth of information about feeding and caring for all those healthy babies. All but one had two young children, and they felt that what they had learned would be of value to new mothers and other mothers with young children. So they decided to write a book that would contain the kind of practical, down-to-earth recipes and advice they wished they had when they brought their babies home.

VICKI LANSKY is a nationally known authority on parenting and has written three bestselling books on children's nutrition: FEED ME! I'M YOURS, THE TAMING OF THE C.A.N.D.Y. MONSTER and FAT-PROOFING YOUR CHILDREN, as well as over a dozen other popular books that have reached millions of parents. She is both a regular featured columnist in SESAME STREET Magazine and the H.E.L.P. columnist for FAMILY CIRCLE Magazine, and excerpts from her books have appeared in many national women's and parenting magazines. She is the mother of two, and lives in suburban Minneapolis.

Our special thanks go to Jeannette Stresemann Honan, R.H., pediatric nurse associate at the Wayzata Children's Clinic, for her time and suggestions in putting this book together.

Contents

Introduction

Welcome to the world of the "haves"—children, that is—and those umpteen new responsibilities, joys, anxieties, precious moments and sleepless nights.

With your first child comes a new and demanding role: nurturing a totally dependent person. What you feed your child helps determine his or her mental and physical health. No one food contains all the nutrients we need, in the amounts we need, so we must opt for a variety of foods representing each of the four basic food groups. They are:

- Meat, fish, poultry, eggs and other protein foods
- Milk and dairy products
- Fruits and vegetables
- Breads and cereals

A good diet is low in refined carbohydrates and refined sugars. Natural carbohydrates and sugars appear in fruits, flours, cereal and vegetables. If your diet is varied, your body will get what it needs.

Americans are often overfed but undernourished. The American diet contains far more calories than the body needs. The empty calories in foods made primarily of refined sugars squeeze the nutritious foods out of our diet. And even when we think we're watching our sugar intake, many of the grocery products we buy contain hidden sugars. Beware of what goes into those nice, consumer-oriented packages; read the labels of foods you buy. Let sugar be part of your family's balanced diet—just not the major part.

Nurturing includes *providing* a balanced and varied diet for your child, not *determining* the quantities he or she should eat Children's appetites will change with their growth patterns. Each child's metabolism is different, with its own different food requirements. Your child will eat as much as his or her system demands at any time if you provide enough varied food at appropriate intervals. Only when your children are old enough to buy penny candy and junk food must you take care that nutritious foods aren't pushed out of their diet.

Your attitude toward food can encourage your child to develop a healthy attitude that can become a lifelong good habit. In fact, your attitude is the key to feeding this new child of yours.

> **Be flexible. Respect strong food dislikes. And remember,**
>
> **Love is not equal to the amount of food your child eats.**

Baby Food From Scratch

Economy, increased nutritional awareness and a "back-to-nature" philosophy are some of the reasons why many parents are making their own baby food. Others discover that making baby food at home is much simpler and less time-consuming than they'd imagined. It can be gratifying to provide your infant with meals that save money (up to 50 percent), are free of additives and fillers, and are as fresh and nutritious as the foods you serve the rest of your family.

You don't have to be a purist to make your own baby food. You probably won't stop using processed baby foods altogether, so when you purchase those little jars, read the labels carefully. Stay with the basic fruits, vegetables and strained meats. Avoid combination and junior meals: you get less protein per serving in those than if you combined a jar of meat and a jar of vegetables yourself. Avoid jars containing sugar and modified starches as major ingredients. Forget the baby desserts; babies don't need them any more than we do.

After a ripe, mashed banana, probably the most commonly recommended first food is instant rice cereal. It has no allergic properties and is usually iron-fortified. The flaked, dry baby food now on the shelves is nutritionally equivalent to baby food in jars. It can be useful, particularly when traveling, as it is lightweight and you only mix the amount your baby needs.

If you are nervous about making your own baby food, start with some of the many soft or pureed grocery store foods available to you down the *other* aisles. These include unsweetened applesauce, canned pumpkin, plain yogurt, cottage cheese (which may need a little extra mashing), banana (the riper it is the more digestible it is), and Cream of Rice cereal. A mashed baked potato (thinned with formula or milk) is also a fine first food.

Don't be in a hurry to start your baby on solid foods. Milk (either mother's milk or formula) is a more important food than solids for the first half of your baby's first year. While the "breast is best," the American Academy of Pediatrics recommends that babies on formula drink an iron-fortified brand until they are 12 months old. Babies younger than one year get most of their vitamins and minerals from breast milk or formula. When solid foods are first introduced, they supplement, but don't replace breast milk or formula.

For the full-term newborn, mother's milk or formula provides all the necessary nutrients. Even after the first four or five months, milk continues to be very important. Solid foods are often introduced at four, five or six months. Solids may be given earlier if you want to accustom your infant to a spoon or to new tastes. Or if you want to satisfy the extra-hungry child.

The introduction of solid food is a red-letter day in your child's life. He or she may not be grateful or even cooperative at first. Don't worry. Food is a great self-reinforcer.

If you find yourself spooning food into a mouth that is pushing the food back out, then your baby is still in the sucking reflex stage and is not really ready for solid foods. Read this as a sign of what your baby's body is telling you, not as a rejection of your fine efforts.

On the other hand, if your baby is grabbing food off your plate, it's time to start new foods and textures. (Actually, you're probably a bit late.)

Check with your doctor before trying new foods and introduce them to your baby one at a time, at one-week intervals, to detect any source of allergic reaction. A few spoonfuls at first will usually suffice. Signs of food intolerance include vomiting, gassiness, diarrhea and skin rash.

If you are doubtful:

- **Follow your pediatrician's preference.** Babies prosper under as many different schedules as there are pediatricians. You also have to "live with" your pediatrician. (If you have definite opinions on the subject, check out several doctors' opinions before choosing one.)

- **Follow your own instincts.** Babies prosper under as many different schedules as there are mothers. (If, on the other hand, your baby is *not* prospering, return to the previous paragraph.)

Whether you feed solids before or after breast or bottle depends on your baby's preference. Some babies need a little milk first to take the edge off their hunger so that they relax enough to be spoon-fed. Start by feeding solid foods once or twice a day, in the morning or evening.

Many doctors recommend withholding egg white, citrus fruits and even some wheat products until a child is past one year of age as they may cause an allergic reaction, especially in food-sensitive families.

Something To Cook In

Clean pots and appliances are all you need for cooking your baby's foods. A crock pot, a pressure cooker and a microwave oven can also be helpful. No, don't go out and buy them. Just use them if you have them.

Steaming fruits and vegetables is best because many nutrients are often lost in cooking water. Inexpensive steamer baskets that collapse to fit most pans work well, but make sure the pot you use has a tight-fitting lid to keep the steam in.

Something To Puree With

By pureeing the unseasoned food *you* eat, you will accustom your baby to the table foods he or she will eat soon.

Your fork can be used to puree, but some of the following might be more efficient:

- A **blender** can quickly and easily puree almost any food into the finest consistency. You will find that vegetables puree best in larger quantities and meats in smaller quantities. In general, you will be using the highest speeds to create a fine puree for the younger baby. As your baby grows, you can proceed to slower speeds for a coarser consistency. Blenders are reasonably priced and useful for making various other child-oriented foods, such as shakes and homemade peanut butter. And you can also use a blender to reconstitute powdered milk or frozen orange juice concentrate. Pureed vegetables can be hidden in meat loaf or spaghetti sauce. The special Mini-Blend containers available from Oster are especially handy for pureeing small quantities of food and storing them in the same container.

- **Food processors** can also be used to puree foods for baby. If you have one, wonderful, but if you don't, this use alone probably does not justify the expense.

- You may have, or wish to buy, **a standard food mill.** These are available in large or small sizes. You place food in the basket; as you turn the handle, the blade presses the food through the holes in the bottom of the basket. The food mill strains most cooked foods to a smooth consistency. Meat and poultry, however, will have a slightly coarser texture.

- The **baby food grinder**, a smaller version of the food mill, has simplified pureeing small amounts of fresh food for your baby. The food fits in a well; you place the turning disc on top. As you turn the handle and press down, the pureed food comes to the top and can be served right from the grinder. The grinder's small size makes it convenient to take along when you travel or eat out. It will grind fruits, vegetables and soft-cooked meats. The grinder conveniently sifts out the skins of peas and the hulls of corn—the hard-to-digest parts.

After your baby outgrows the need for pureed food, you will find the grinder convenient for: chopping nuts, grinding raisins and other dried fruits, softening butter or margarine, making egg salad, mashing a banana, mashing a baked or boiled potato, grating soft cheese, and probably many more uses.

Baby food grinders are usually available in the baby departments of retail stores.

Handling and Storing Foods

Proper handling is important when you make your own baby food.

- Work with clean hands and clean utensils (including grinders and cutting boards).

- Prepare a food immediately after removing it from the refrigerator and freeze any leftovers or volume foods immediately.

Any open jars of commercial baby food can be stored in the refrigerator for two to three days. Commercial baby food manufacturers do not recommend using the container as a serving dish because the baby's saliva on the spoon contaminates the food in the jar and speeds up the spoiling process. Another reason to avoid feeding a baby directly from the jar is the tendency to finish the jar and thus overfeed your baby. Plus, by transferring it to a serving dish, you can also check the product for any foreign matter.

When making more food than will be eaten in just one meal, you need a way to store the larger volume safely. Freezing your own foods gives you the variety and convenience of prepared foods. You will find it easy to cook in volume. You can always keep an adequate supply on hand and never need to rush to prepare food for a hungry baby.

You can easily freeze meal-sized portions for your baby using one of two methods: the "Food Cube" method and the "Plop" method. As your baby's appetite grows you can add more cubes per meal or make bigger "plops." Before a meal, take out the food you want to serve. Thaw it in the refrigerator or warm the food in a warming dish or in an egg poacher cup over boiling water. Remember that cold food and milk are acceptable to your baby, even if not to you. Their taste buds are not fully developed, so foods that seem warm to you may seem hot to your baby.

The "Food Cube" Method

Pour prepared, pureed food into plastic, pop-out ice cube trays. Freeze immediately. Pop out the frozen cubes and transfer them to plastic freezer bags. Label and date. The food cubes can be stored up to two months.

The "Plop" Method

Plop pureed or finely ground foods by the spoonful onto a cookie sheet. The size of each "plop" depends on how much you think the baby will eat at one meal. Freeze immediately. Transfer frozen "plops" to plastic bags. Label and date. "Plops" can be stored up to two months.

A cube or a "plop" travels well for short journeys. By the time you've arrived, baby's meal is defrosted and ready to be eaten.

Food can be frozen in empty, clean baby-food jars. Be careful not to fill them completely, because food will expand while freezing. Small Tupperware jars with lids can serve the same purpose. They stack easily in the freezer, too.

Keep protein foods, cereals, vegetables and fruits in separate containers.

Baby's Cereals

Cereals are the typical first foods given to babies because they are fortified with an iron babies can absorb readily. You will find the commercial instant baby cereals both convenient and nutritious. Rice cereal is commonly recommended first, since it is easy on most all digestive tracts. But you can also easily make whole grain and unprocessed cereals, such as Cream of Wheat and Wheatena. You can even run oatmeal through your blender before cooking for a finer cereal. It pays to make these cereals in quantity and freeze the balance by the methods previously described.

Hints: When preparing cereals for your baby, keep in mind:

- A nursing mother may add expressed milk to cereals (or any foods) to make them more readily accepted, as the smell and taste are familiar to the baby.

- Any cereal can be sweetened with pureed fruits or a bit of brown sugar or molasses.

- Add a little plain yogurt to hot cereal. It gives a creamy texture to grainy cereals.

For cereal recipes, see page 52.

Baby's Fruits

All fresh fruits, except bananas, must be cooked until they are soft—at least until your baby is about six to seven months old.

Canned fruits, packed in their own juice, are also easy to puree and serve. If it comes in a sugar syrup, drain and rinse before using.

Banana

Use one medium-size, fully ripe (speckled skin) banana. Cut it in half and peel one half to use. Cover the remaining half (in the peel) and store in the refrigerator for up to two days. Mash the half banana with a fork or put it through a baby food grinder. The riper the banana, the more digestible it is for the baby. You can also peel ripe bananas, wrap them tightly in meal-size portions and freeze. When ready to use, thaw and use immediately.

Other Fruits

Apples, peaches, pears, plums and apricots can be prepared in one of two methods.

Water Method: Wash fruit, peel and cut into small pieces. Add ¼ cup boiling water to 1 cup of fruit. Simmer until tender (10-20 minutes). Don't add sugar; babies prefer the natural sweetness of fruit. Blend or puree until smooth. Refrigerate what you will use that day and freeze the balance.

Steam Method: Wash fruit well, remove skin and steam for 15-20 minutes. Cool. Remove pits. Blend or puree until smooth. Refrigerate what you will use that day and freeze the balance.

Cottage Cheese Fruit

½ cup cottage cheese
½ cup fresh, raw or cooked
    fruit
4 to 6 tablespoons orange juice

Blend quickly and serve cool. Using this recipe, you can incorporate one of your prepared fruits into a whole meal.

Tropical Treat

½ very ripe avocado, mashed
    or pureed
½ very ripe banana, mashed or
    pureed
¼ cup cottage cheese or
    yogurt

Combine all ingredients.

Homemade Fruit Gelatin

Make your own fruit gelatin by dissolving 1 envelope unflavored gelatin in ¼ cup warm water. Add 1 cup pureed fruit and chill.

Baby's Vegetables

Fresh vegetables should be used whenever possible for best nutrition, flavor and economy. Frozen vegetables are your best substitute for fresh. Canned vegetables, while not as nutritious, are still convenient and worthwhile; they are already cooked and need only be pureed. (Use the liquid from the can, if possible, because many nutrients are in it.)

Basic Vegetable Recipe

Cook beets, carrots, sweet potatoes, peas, green beans and potatoes by one of two methods.

Water Method: Peel and slice for fast cooking or use frozen. Cook in 1 to 1½ inches of water 20 minutes. Puree or blend with some of the cooking water or orange juice.

Steam Method: Peel and slice for fast cooking or use frozen. Steam over boiling water until tender. Puree or blend, adding cooking water for right consistency.

Baked Sweet Potato and Apples

¾ cup cooked sweet potato
¼ cup liquid (milk, cooking
    water)
1 cup applesauce or apples

Preheat oven to 350°. Peel, core and slice apples. Mix sweet potatoes and apples in buttered baking dish. Pour liquid over. Cover and bake for 30 minutes. Puree or mash with a fork.

Vegetable/Egg Yolk Custard

¼ cup vegetable puree
    (carrots, peas, etc.)
1 egg yolk, beaten

¼ cup milk
½ teaspoon brown sugar
    (optional)

Preheat oven to 350°. Blend all ingredients; pour into two custard cups and place in a pan of water. Bake for 30 minutes. Refrigerate up to three days.

Vegetable Soup

¼ cup cooked pureed
    vegetables
1 tablespoon butter or
    margarine

1 tablespoon whole wheat or
    white flour
¼ cup liquid (water, broth or
    milk)

Combine in a saucepan until warm.

Baby's Meats and Poultry

You can use any meat you have cooked for your family, or cook up to a month's supply of meat for your baby at a time, and puree it. If you want a smoother consistency, mix meat with a small cooked serving of Cream of Rice and some milk and butter. Even a little water or juice will help pureeing in a blender. Combine chicken with a little banana and milk to get a smooth-textured meal. Meats cooked in a crock pot (minus seasonings) are tender and easy to puree.

All-Purpose Meat Stew

⅓ cup flour
1½ pounds stew meat in 1-inch cubes
2 tablespoons oil
3 cups water

4 medium potatoes
5 medium carrots
1 package (10 ounce) frozen peas

Coat meat with flour and brown in oil. Add water and cover pan tightly. Simmer 1½ hours. Scrub, peel and cube potatoes and carrots; add to meat. Simmer 15 minutes. Add peas and simmer 5 minutes. Puree. Makes 4 to 5 cups.

Variation: Use any vegetable or ½ cup rice as a substitute for the potatoes.

Chicken Liver Special

1 carrot, chopped
1 small onion, chopped

2 stalks celery, chopped
½ pound chicken livers

Steam vegetables in a small amount of water until tender (10 minutes). Steam livers until they change color. Chop coarsely. Puree vegetables and their liquid with the meat in a blender or food mill.

Pineapple Chicken

Combine boiled or baked chicken meat in a blender with canned, drained pineapple that was packed in its own juice. For a snack drink, strain the drained juice, mix it with water and serve.

Cockadoodle Stew

1 cup cubed chicken (or turkey), cooked
¼ cup rice, cooked

¼ cup vegetables, cooked
¼ cup chicken broth
¼ cup milk

Blend or puree together and make into food cubes or "plops." (See section on proper storage, page 7.)

Good substitutes for meat and poultry include cottage cheese, boneless fish, cheese, cooked egg yolks, macaroni and cheese.

Important

These recipes do not require extra salt. Studies indicate that excess salt contributes to hypertension in later life. Since a taste for salty food is acquired, you can help your child avoid the risks of salt by minimizing it in his or her diet.

Yogurt

Try it; you'll like it! Yogurt is an ideal early baby food. Once your baby can take whole-milk products, yogurt should be first on your list. It is easily digestible. You may not be used to yogurt yourself, but this is an excellent time to experiment. If you don't like it, your baby is sure to finish off the container for you.

Start with plain yogurt. It can be used as a base for fruits (such as mashed banana) or cereals, or even those little jars of baby-food fruits. Yogurt can also be used instead of sour cream or buttermilk for cooking.

Beverages

These beverages make good meal supplements or snacks. They can be served in a bottle or glass, for baby or toddler, and even for Mom and Dad.

When your baby graduates to regular cow's milk, avoid skim milk until your child is at least two years old. Nutritionists feel that those butterfats in the milk are essential for growth in young children.

Hint: Extra formula, when baby graduates to milk, can be used for cooking, baking or even in coffee.

Some of the following recipes call for eggs, which is a good way of serving eggs to those children for whom "egg" means, "Forget it!" Most physicians don't recommend serving egg (cooked or raw) to babies under six months or even to babies under one year old, since some infants have an allergic reaction to egg white. Try using the yolk only, and freeze the white for later use in baking.

Because raw eggs (the shells, actually) can be a carrier of the bacteria salmonella, they are not a good choice for infants younger than nine to twelve months old. Their stomachs are much more sensitive to the effects of this bacteria.

Honey Alert

Avoid the use of honey in beverages and uncooked foods for infants younger than one year. There is concern that infants can't handle certain botulism toxins that are sometimes found in honey. If these drinks aren't sweet enough with the pureed fruits, it is better to add sugar instead of honey.

Yogurt Milkshake

1 cup plain yogurt
1 cup orange juice

1 ripe banana
2 tablespoons honey (optional)

Blend.

Carrot Juice

1 pound carrots (4 to 5
    medium)
1 quart water
½ cup non-fat dry milk

If your little one can't quite handle apple or citrus juices, even when diluted, consider this recipe. Wash the carrots and chop into small pieces. Place all the ingredients in a tightly covered pot and bring to a boil. Simmer for 1 hour. Cool and strain. Serve in a bottle with an enlarged nipple hole. Store juice in the refrigerator for up to seven days. It can also be frozen in food cubes.

Variation: In a blender, combine one jar of strained baby carrots and two cups of water. Add one teaspoon of sweetener. Blend until well mixed. Store in the refrigerator.

Banana Smoothie

1½ cups milk
1 large banana

¼ teaspoon vanilla
1 tablespoon honey (optional)

Blend and serve at once.

The banana you use can also be one that has been peeled and frozen, giving you a use for that last ripe banana.

Sunny Sipper

½ cup orange juice
3 tablespoons lemon juice
1 can (13 ounce) evaporated
    milk

1 can (13 ounce) apricot nectar
½ cup honey (optional)

Blend, serve chilled.

Milk Eggnog

1 cup cold milk
1 egg
¼ teaspoon vanilla

1 tablespoon honey (optional)
non-fat dry milk (optional)

Blend. Eggnog is another way of providing a good protein for your older toddler who has decided to abstain from most of the protein foods you are offering. Fortify with several tablespoons non-fat dry milk if you wish.

Variation: Orange juice may be substituted for the milk.

Orange Delight

1 to 2 eggs
⅓ cup orange juice
    concentrate
¼ cup non-fat dry milk

½ banana (or equivalent fruit)
¾ cup water
ice

Mix in blender. The more ice you add, the slushier the drink becomes.

Milk Marvels

Add one of the following to 1 cup cold milk to add nutrition and interest. Mix well in a blender:

- ½ banana, mashed or frozen.

- One scoop of fruit-flavored ice cream or sherbet.

- ½ cup frozen strawberries plus the syrup or ½ cup fresh berries plus sugar.

- ½ cup of any fresh, bruised berries; 2 tablespoons sugar, 1 tablespoon lemon or orange juice.

- ½ banana, a scoop of vanilla ice cream and 1 tablespoon chocolate syrup.

- Canned peaches or pears, 2 tablespoons fruit syrup and 1 scoop vanilla ice cream.

Fortified Milk

The protein value of milk can be increased by adding some non-fat dry milk to regular milk. But do so only in moderation, especially if your child already has a low fluid intake.

Hint: For the child who refuses milk, remember that it can be "eaten" in the form of puddings, custards, cheese, yogurt or creamy soups.

Hints for the do-it-yourself (at last!) drinker:

- Fill a glass only about ⅓ full to limit waste when the inevitable spills occur. Provide refills when requested.

- Have your child practice drinking water from a cup while he or she is taking a bath.

- Cut straws down to size for the child and the cup or glass being used.

Finger Foods

Good health depends on sound eating habits. What your child eats and how he or she eats is established in the earliest years.

Finger foods should be introduced when your child's eye-hand coordination has matured enough that he or she is able to pick up objects with fingers or a spoon and get them to his or her mouth. At approximately six to eight months, when your child is able to sit in a high chair and can reach for objects, a graham cracker, a few Cheerios or a piece of soft cheese will be of great interest. If you allow your baby to experiment with food (despite the mess), you will have fewer problems in the long run. The more you allow your child to do, the faster he or she will learn. Don't be surprised if you need two spoons per meal—one for your child and one for you!

Be sure to supply the proper equipment: a high chair, a spoon with a bowl small enough to fit the baby's mouth and a handle short enough for the baby to control, and an unbreakable cup with two handles and a weighted bottom (which may save you time cleaning up the floor). Speaking of floors, you may want to use newspapers or a plastic tablecloth under the high chair to save you the three-times-a-day cleanup.

A child needs far less food than many parents expect. A child eats when hungry, and will take just what is needed to maintain the proper growth rate. Servings should be small, to avoid being discouraging; so should the plates or bowls. Add new foods gradually. If your child should reject a particular food, return to a favorite and offer the new food again in a few days. It isn't always easy to respect your child's strong food dislikes, but it is important to try. Don't fret! Don't nag!

At around one year of age, your child's appetite will decrease because the growth spurt of that first year slows down. Despite knowing this, it still comes as a surprise when children refuse to eat or finish foods they enjoyed or wolfed down just the week or months before. Toddlers change their food likes from day to day and meal to meal, so remember to offer old favorites and previously refused foods from time to time. Some children cling to the personal service of being fed, but ultimately (given the opportunity) they all learn to feed themselves.

Finger Foods *Not* Recommended for Babies Younger Than Twelve to Eighteen Months Old

Difficult To Digest	May Cause Gagging
Bacon rind	Hot dogs, whole
Baked beans	Grapes, whole
Chocolate	Hard candies
Corn	Ice cubes
Cucumbers	Nuts and raisins
Leafy vegetables	Olives
Onion, uncooked	Popcorn

Serve toast sticks, bread sticks and raw carrot sticks with caution to very young children. Also, peanut butter should be used sparingly or thinned with milk for very young children so it will not stick in the back of the mouth and cause gagging.

Nuts and popcorn are *not* recommended even for older toddlers! Some children are more susceptible to gagging than others but all children have smaller airways and weaker gag reflexes than adults.

Finger foods should be eaten only when your child is sitting up—not while running and not while lying down—and only when an adult is supervising.

Now that you know what specific finger foods to avoid or serve with care, here are several lists of ideas for foods that children *can* handle as they grow older.

Finger Foods Appropriate for Babies Six to Eight Months Old

Applesauce
Arrowroot cookies
Bananas, mashed or in small slices
Canned pears and peaches
Cheerios
Chicken liver and other tender meat, mashed or chopped
Cooked cereals
Cottage cheese
Graham crackers
Ground meat (may or may not be accepted)
Potatoes, mashed
Pudding
Soft-cooked vegetables, mashed
Toast, lightly buttered
Vanilla ice cream
Yogurt, frozen or regular

Finger Foods Appropriate for Babies Nine Months to One Year Old

Bagel, soft
Carrots and other vegetables, cooked soft
Cheeses, soft
Chicken, in soft-cooked pieces
Custards, soft
Egg, boiled, scrambled or poached (yolks only if your child is
    sensitive)
Egg noodles
Fish, without bones (also gefilte fish)
Macaroni pasta
Meatballs, tiny ones
Meats, tender varieties of lamb, veal and beef
Orange sections, peeled with loose membrane removed
Peaches, ripe and peeled
Rice
Spaghetti with meat sauce
Toast

Texture becomes of great interest at this point. Most babies with two to four teeth are receptive to lumpier foods. Regardless of age, babies do not need teeth to chew; gums do an adequate job on soft foods. Chewier fruits and vegetables should be added as more teeth erupt. It is easy to drift into the habit of serving only soft fruits and vegetables, but it is wise to gradually increase the chewy foods as your baby's chewing ability increases.

Finger Foods Appropriate for Babies One Year and Older

Vegetables
Asparagus tips
Avocado, ripe
Broccoli tips
Carrot sticks, preferably soft-cooked or grated
Cauliflower
Celery, with all strands removed
Cherry tomatoes, halved
French fries
Green beans
Lettuce, cut up
Mushrooms
Peas, uncooked and frozen ones too!
Pickle spears
Potatoes, mashed
Sweet potato, cooked and mashed
Tomatoes, peeled

Fruit
Apples, peeled
Banana, whole or cut into sections
Blueberries
Cantaloupe, cut into bite-size pieces
Dried fruits
Fruit cocktail, canned
Grapes, halved for young toddlers
Mandarin oranges, canned
Navel oranges, peeled and sectioned
Peaches, peeled
Pears, peeled
Strawberries, halved
Sweet cherries, pitted
Watermelon, pitted and cut into bite-size pieces

Dairy

Cottage cheese (add fresh or canned fruit for interest)
Deviled eggs made with mayonnaise
Hard-cooked eggs
Small squares of soft cheese, such as American or Gouda
Yogurt (may be served semi-frozen)

Meats

*Bacon, crisp
*Beef jerky
Chicken or beef liver
Chicken or turkey, diced
*Frankfurters, fresh (see note below)
*Ham, cut into bite-size pieces
Hamburger (try it in different shapes, such as sticks)
Lamb chops (with a bone that has no sharp points)
*Luncheon meats
Meatballs, small ones
Roasts, tender cuts (may grind)
*Sausage
Spareribs, well cooked
Tuna fish
Turkey, ground and cooked like hamburger
Veal

*These meats contain sodium nitrites (which act as a preservative and coloring agent). They should be served in moderation. Some experts question the nutritional safety of nitrites but of even greater concern is the large amount of fat and cholesterol these foods add to a child's diet.

TAKE CARE

Since hot dogs have been the most common cause of food-related choking among children younger than two years of age, monitor your child's consumption of them carefully. Better yet, slice a hot dog lengthwise—turn—and slice lengthwise again, before serving alone or on a bun.

Breads, Cereals and Other Grains
  Arrowroot cookies
  Bagel and cream cheese
  Bran muffins, slightly frozen
  Cereals, cold (dry or with milk)
  Cereals, hot (regular or instant)
  Graham crackers
  Macaroni, cooked (a variety of shapes)
  Oyster crackers
  Pretzel rods (minus excess salt)
  Saltines
  Sandwiches, broken into small pieces
  Spaghetti, cooked
  Spinach noodles (those green ones)
  Toast, lightly buttered and cut into fourths
  Triscuits
  Zwieback

Avoid those ready-to-eat cereals that are sugar-frosted, honey-coated or chocolate-flavored. They add more unnecessary sugars to your child's diet.

As your child's ability with a spoon increases, so should the variety of bowl-type food you serve. Be patient and try not to let the lack of neatness dissuade you from letting your child continue to practice.

Teething

This early-life passage may be quiet or traumatic. Try slightly stale bagels, a frozen banana on a stick, the hard core of a pineapple or a frozen food cube on a stick. Cold washcloths are good non-food teethers. Chilled pacifiers can be soothing, too.

Recipes for Teething Biscuits and Crackers

You can harden almost any bread by baking it in a very low oven (150-200°) for 15-20 minutes. Your baby will enjoy teething on a variety of hard breads—such as whole wheat and rye—that you can make this way. But you may also like to try some of the following for economy and nutrition.

Hard Round Teething Biscuits

2 eggs
1 cup sugar (white or brown)
2 to 2½ cups flour (white,
    whole wheat or a
    combination)

Break eggs into a bowl and stir until creamy. Add sugar and continue to stir. Gradually add enough flour to make a stiff dough. Roll out between two sheets of lightly floured wax paper to about ¾-inch thickness.

Cut in round shapes. Place on a lightly greased cookie sheet. Let it stand overnight (10-12 hours). Bake at 325° until browned and hard. This will make about 12 durable and almost crumb-free teething biscuits.

Banana Bread Sticks

¼ cup brown sugar
½ cup oil
2 eggs
1 cup banana, mashed

1¾ cup flour (white, whole
    wheat or a combination)
2 teaspoons baking powder
½ teaspoon baking soda

Combine ingredients and stir only until smooth. Pour into a greased loaf pan. Bake about 1 hour or until firmly set at 350°. Cool, remove from pan and cut into sticks. Spread out on a cookie sheet and bake at 150° for 1 hour or longer until the sticks are hard and crunchy. Store in a tightly covered container.

Oatmeal Crackers

3 cups oatmeal, uncooked
1 cup wheat germ
2 cups flour (white, whole
    wheat or a combination)

3 tablespoons sugar
¾ cup oil
1 cup water

Combine ingredients and roll onto two cookie sheets. Cut into squares. Bake for 30 minutes at 300° or until crisp. Be sure to roll thin and bake well.

Enriched Teething Biscuits

1 egg yolk, beaten
3 tablespoons honey
1 teaspoon vanilla
1½ tablespoons oil
¼ cup liquid milk
1 tablespoon uncooked
   oatmeal

1 cup flour (white, whole wheat
   or a combination)
1 tablespoon soy flour
1 tablespoon wheat germ
1 tablespoon non-fat dry milk

Blend egg yolk, honey, vanilla, liquid milk and oil. Then add dry ingredients. Dough should be stiff. Roll dough thin and cut into finger-length rectangles or desired shapes. Bake at 350° on an ungreased cookie sheet for 15 minutes. Cool and store in an airtight container.

Variation: While the last three ingredients enrich the recipe, if you don't have them on hand, the recipe still works.

Homemade Graham Crackers

1 cup flour (graham or whole
   wheat)
1 cup unbleached flour
1 teaspoon baking powder

¼ cup margarine or butter
½ cup honey
¼ cup milk

Combine flours and baking powder. Cut in butter or margarine until consistency of cornmeal. Stir in honey. Add milk to make a stiff dough.

Roll out on floured surface to ¼-inch thickness. Cut into squares. Prick with a fork. Brush with milk. Bake at 400° on an ungreased baking sheet for 18 minutes or until golden brown. If rolled thicker, these crackers can be used as teething biscuits, or use in Quick Graham Cracker Dessert (page 33).

Toddler Food

Even though your toddler is now on table foods, you will probably notice that your meals are more often geared toward what your child will eat than the other way around. Save your gourmet delights for a few more years.

Lunch

Children have been known to survive eating only peanut butter and jelly sandwiches (or whatever) for extended periods of time. But if you're simply out of ideas, you may want to consider some of the following. Try serving them on extra-thin bread, or regular bread, sliced thin (while partially frozen).

Lunch Ideas

Deviled Ham—Spread on graham cracker or whole wheat bread.

Cream Cheese—Spread on graham crackers. Very popular.

Egg Salad—Add mayonnaise for desired consistency. Finely chopped or grated celery may also be added.

Tuna Salad—Mash with a fork or put in a blender (depending on desired consistency). Mix with mayonnaise.

Lunch-in-a-Cone—Serve tuna salad, egg salad, yogurt or cottage cheese in an ice cream cone.

Full of Baloney—Fill slices of baloney with cottage cheese or spread with cream cheese and roll.

Chicken Salad—Mix cubes of chicken with mayonnaise, finely chopped celery and grated carrot.

Triangle Sandwiches—Spread whole wheat bread with raspberry jam and top with thin slices of banana. Cut sandwich diagonally into fourths (triangles).

Cottage Cheese Salad—Combine 1 can crushed pineapple, 1 cup cottage cheese, Dream Whip and a 3-ounce package of lime Jell-O (either partially jelled or simply sprinkled on).

Hint: Set gelatin more quickly by substituting 1 cup ice cubes for 1 cup cold water.

French Toast—Substitute orange juice or condensed soup for the milk.

Leftover Meat Sandwiches—Blend about ¾ cup cubed meat, 1 hard-boiled egg, 1 tablespoon butter and 1 tablespoon milk to make a paste. Keep in an airtight container in the refrigerator. (Pureed meat from baby food jars can also be used as a sandwich spread.)

Grilled Cheese Sandwich—Place 1 to 2 pieces of American cheese between 2 slices of bread. Brown on both sides in 1 tablespoon margarine in a skillet.

Deviled Eggs—Add a face by using raisins for eyes, nose and mouth.

Other Appealing Lunch Ideas

Peanut butter is a staple in most homes with young children. Do purchase those brands in the refrigerated section of your grocery store or those labeled "natural" where the oil has risen to the top, since the hydrogenated oil in the shelf-stable varieties is heavier and less healthful. Check the ingredients on the shelf-stable ones too. A few additions can make those sandwiches more imaginative and nutritious:

- Peanut butter and ground raisins mixed with fruit juice.
- Peanut butter and grated raw carrots.
- Peanut butter topped with applesauce.
- Peanut butter topped with artificial bacon bits plus honey.
- Peanut butter and banana slices.
- Peanut butter and cream cheese, blended with 2 tablespoons orange juice or honey.

Other ideas for a quick and nutritious sandwich for both parent and child include the following:

- Cream cheese with jelly.
- Cream cheese with ground raisins.
- Cream cheese with peeled and finely chopped (or grated) cucumber.
- Chopped egg, cheese and bacon.
- Ground leftovers, eggs and pickle relish.
- Cottage cheese with grated pineapple.
- Cottage cheese topped with sliced hard-boiled egg.

Keeping the bread in the freezer keeps it from tearing when the peanut butter or cream cheese is spread. It thaws in only a few minutes.

Fill an empty ice cube tray with finger foods such as fresh strawberries, cheese cubes, lunch meat, hard-cooked egg wedges and carrot sticks. Do this early in the day and refrigerate until serving time, when it will provide an interesting treat for some hard-to-please toddler.

For the younger set who are ready to eat corn-on-the-cob but not digest it, slice off the tops of the kernels, or slice down the middles of each row of kernels so the corn can be sucked out.

Homemade Alphabet Soup

1 teaspoon alphabet noodles	dash of salt
2 teaspoons instant tapioca	butter
⅔ cup vegetable broth	

Cook over high heat for 3 minutes, stirring constantly. Remove from heat, stir in a dash of salt and a dot of butter.

"Making-your-own-lunch" (or sandwich) often helps get a food eaten.

Dinner

One of dinnertime's biggest problems is that your child's stomach is inevitably half-an-hour to an hour ahead of your meal schedule. You can feed your child early and avoid the next hour's headache. Or try one of the following if you are determined that the whole family will eat together.

Offer a salad, side dish or carrot as an appetizer. An ice cube can occupy an older child for a fairly long time. Serve it in a plastic cup. Sugarless gum or bubblegum may work. (Regarding gum, the concept of chewing versus swallowing begins at about eighteen months, although your child will "lose" many pieces before the idea catches hold.)

And do you find that your child simply can't sit still during the meal? He or she must stand, bounce, climb, kick the table, go to the toilet and generally drive you bananas. We can offer no remedy—only sympathy, for you are not alone. (We probably performed these same foul deeds as kids ourselves.)

Hint: An ice cube can bring many foods to an edible temperature quickly. Toddlers are not in favor of foods hot from the stove or oven.

Dinner Ideas

Tiny Meatballs—Add beaten eggs, oatmeal or wheat germ and grated cheese.

Meat Loafies—Add ingredients above, but cook in a muffin tin. (Freezes well in this form. Reheat on a cookie sheet in oven or toaster oven.)

Macaroni and Cheese—Serve your combo or the grocer's. An all-time favorite.

Chicken Livers—Saute in butter until tender; cut into pieces. Or wrap in bacon and broil.

Boned Fish—Use only fish that is quite fleshy, such as cod. Always check carefully for bones.

Corned Beef Hash—Place in a frying pan. Make a depression with the back of a spoon and break an egg into it. Cover and heat until egg has settled. Messy with fingers, but not bad with a spoon.

Pineapple Franks—Split frankfurters and fill with drained pineapple; broil for 5 to 10 minutes. Older toddlers enjoy these.

Omelettes—Whether your child likes this plain or with such additions as onions, green pepper, cheese, wheat germ or others, it should be cooked as a large pancake rather than scrambled. It is much easier for a child to eat this when it can be broken into pieces.

Dinner Recipes

Tuna Burgers

1 can (7 ounce) tuna, drained
2 tablespoons onion, chopped
2 tablespoons pickle, chopped
¼ cup mayonnaise
slice of cheese (optional)

Combine ingredients. Split and toast hamburger buns, and spread bottom half with tuna mixture. Top with a slice of cheese and broil for 4 minutes or until cheese melts. Add bun toppers.

Tuna Patties

⅔ cup Grape-Nuts
½ cup milk
1 cup onion, finely chopped
2 cans (7 ounces each) tuna, drained
2 tablespoons shortening
2 eggs, slightly beaten
1 teaspoon lemon juice

Add cereal to milk; set aside. Saute onions in 1 tablespoon shortening until tender but not browned. Add tuna, eggs and lemon juice to cereal mixture. Blend thoroughly. Form 12 patties. Brown on both sides in 1 tablespoon shortening.

Salmon Souffle

1 can (16 ounce) salmon
1 can (7¾ ounce) evaporated
    milk
3 tablespoons butter
3 tablespoons flour

½ teaspoon dry mustard
4 eggs, separated
paprika (optional)

Drain salmon liquid into 8-ounce measuring cup and add enough milk to make 1 cup. Flake salmon and check for bones. In a saucepan, melt butter and blend in flour and dry mustard. Gradually add milk and cook, stirring until thickened. Remove from heat. Stir in beaten egg yolks and salmon; cool. Beat egg whites until stiff and fold into mixture. Pour into buttered 2-quart souffle or casserole dish and bake at 350° for 45-50 minutes. Dust with paprika.

Loafer's Loaf

1 pound ground beef
1¼ cup uncooked oatmeal
¼ cup minced onion
¼ cup American cheese,
    grated

½ teaspoon celery salt
1 cup milk
⅔ cup tomatoes, chopped
1 egg, beaten

Combine all ingredients. Pack into greased loaf pan. Bake at 350° for 1 hour and 10 minutes.

Simple Souffle

¼ cup margarine or butter,
    melted
¼ cup flour
1 cup milk

1 cup cheddar, Swiss or
    mozzarella cheese,
    shredded (optional)
4 eggs
¼ teaspoon cream of tartar

Melt margarine; stir in flour. Cook over medium heat until bubbly. Add milk and stir constantly until smooth and thickened. Add cheese if you are using it. Beat 2 egg yolks until smooth. Blend a little of the hot mixture into the yolk mixture. Return yolk mixture to saucepan and blend. Remove from heat. Pour into 1 ½-quart casserole. Beat 4 egg whites until stiff, not dry, along with cream of tartar. Fold into casserole dish. Bake at 350° for 30-40 minutes. Delicious even when it falls.

Simpler Souffle

1 can condensed cheddar
   cheese soup
6 eggs, yolks and whites
   whipped separately

Combine beaten egg yolks and cheese soup in a casserole dish. Fold in egg whites. Bake at 400° for 40 minutes or until done.

Orange Chicken

2 chicken legs and thighs
2 tablespoons butter, melted

½ cup orange juice
poultry seasoning

Place chicken in small baking dish and season. Mix melted butter with orange juice. Pour over chicken. Sprinkle with poultry seasoning. Bake 15 minutes at 350°. Turn and baste with juice mixture. Broil for 15 minutes or until chicken is crisp and tender.

Chicken Quiche

1 9-inch pie shell, unbaked
½ cup chicken, cooked and
   diced
1½ cups Swiss cheese,
   shredded

3 eggs, slightly beaten
1½ cups milk
2 tablespoons Parmesan
   cheese, grated

Place chicken in pie shell and add Swiss cheese. Combine eggs and milk. Pour over cheese. Sprinkle on Parmesan cheese. Bake at 375° for 30-35 minutes or until a knife inserted into center comes out clean. Allow to stand 10 minutes before serving.

Tasty Vegetables

"If it's green, it must be yucky" is a philosophy you might run into (like a stone wall). Just increase the variety of vegetables in your menus until your child's taste tolerance widens.

One way of introducing your child to a new vegetable, such as an artichoke, is by *not* serving it. "Adults-only" food often becomes more desirable when treated as forbidden fruit. You can "perhaps" let your child have a taste from your plate. Graduating to "adult" foods makes children feel more grown-up and at the very least saves you from throwing out or arguing over some tasty part of your meal.

One method of using up any leftover cooked yellow or white vegetable is to mash it, mix it with an egg and cook it like a pancake or bake it in a muffin tin.

Older toddlers are often fond of nibbling on frozen green peas straight from the freezer bag! Or try Chinese pea pods—they are sweet. Often, too, your child will eat vegetables that he or she picks from your summer garden, while passing over the same item from your refrigerator.

If you're really desperate, try green noodles. They're made with spinach.

Meat loaf and spaghetti sauce can hide pureed vegetables added in moderate amounts. You might even want to try this with hamburgers. Experiment. Do it gradually. Pumpkin pie is yet another way to serve a yellow vegetable.

Raw vegetables often meet with less resistance than those that are cooked. Combine this with the way your toddler attacks the hors d'oeuvres when your company is starting on cocktails and you have:

Raw Vegetables Served With a Dip

Vegetables can include carrots, celery, cauliflower, radishes, cucumber spears, broccoli, sliced zucchini, slivers of green pepper or mushrooms. The dip can have yogurt, sour cream or cheese as a base.

Bunny Food

Combine grated carrots with raisins. Mix with some mayonnaise, or a bit of honey and lemon juice.

Pickled Carrots

Fill finished pickle jars that still have liquid with carrot sticks for a new flavored snack.

Baked Banana

Peel firm bananas and place in a well-greased baking dish. Brush with butter and bake at 350° for 12-15 minutes. Remove from oven. With the tip of a spoon, make a shallow groove the length of the banana and fill with honey.

Honeyed Carrots

3 tablespoons butter
4 cups carrots, sliced
3 tablespoons orange juice

¼ teaspoon ginger
4 tablespoons honey

Combine all ingredients in a saucepan and cover. Cook over low heat for 30 minutes or until tender. Stir occasionally. Leftovers may be frozen.

Un"beet"able Gelatin

1 jar strained baby beets
1 package (3 ounce) straw-
    berry Jell-O

cold water
1 cup boiling water

Chill strained beets thoroughly and combine with cold water to make 1 cup liquid and set aside. Dissolve Jell-O in boiling water and add the liquid beet mixture. Chill until set.

Variation: Substitute cooked and pureed fresh or canned beets for baby food jar equivalent. Beets vary, depending upon the season. For those that are not sweet enough, add 1 teaspoon sugar to beet mixture.

Green Bean Bake

2 packages whole green
    beans, frozen
1 cup sour cream
¼ teaspoon pepper

2 tablespoons butter
1 cup soft bread crumbs
1 garlic clove, sliced (optional)

Cook green beans with garlic following label directions. Drain. Place in baking dish. Stir pepper into sour cream and spoon over beans. Melt butter in small saucepan. Add bread crumbs and toss. Sprinkle over sour cream. Bake at 350° for 20 minutes.

Quick Desserts

Quick Graham Cracker Dessert

Crumble one graham cracker in a bowl. Add a teaspoonful of honey and a bit of warm milk. Mash, mix and serve.

Yogurt Sundae

Put some yogurt (frozen or not) in a dish. Add fresh fruit and pour honey over the fruit. Sprinkle with granola or nuts. Top with a maraschino cherry.

No-Work Dessert

Serve any fruit with separate small bowls of sour cream and brown sugar. Dip the fresh fruit into the brown sugar, then into the sour cream and eat.

Chocolate Cream Cheese

1 tablespoon cream cheese	½ teaspoon sugar
1 teaspoon milk	⅛ teaspoon cocoa

Beat the cheese with the milk until smooth. Then beat in the sugar and cocoa.

Apple Custard

1 apple
1 egg
2 tablespoons sugar

Preheat oven to 350°. Wash, peel and core apple. Slice very thin and sprinkle with sugar. Beat the egg and fold into the apples. Put these into a well-buttered baking dish. Bake for 30 minutes.

Banana and Apple Whip

1 small banana	1 teaspoon milk
1 small apple	¼ teaspoon sugar

Wash, peel and cut apple into small pieces (or grate it). Add the remaining ingredients and beat until blended. Serve immediately.

Banana Instant Pudding

2 ripe bananas, mashed	2 tablespoons peanut butter
½ cup applesauce	2 tablespoons honey

Stir until smooth, chill. Sprinkle with cinnamon or wheat germ before serving.

Homemade Fresh Fruit Sherbet

1¼ cups fresh fruit
1 cup sugar
2 egg whites, beaten

Cut the fruit into small pieces. Mix the fruit and sugar well. Beat egg whites stiff and fold them in. Put in a freezer tray and freeze for about 2 hours, stirring occasionally. Cover with wax paper until ready to serve.

Chocolate "Ice Cream"

½ can sweetened condensed
     milk
1½ tablespoons cocoa
½ cup regular milk

Combine ingredients and freeze for about 3 hours in a freezer tray.

Nutritious Frostings

Base:

2 tablespoons soft butter or
     margarine
¼ cup honey
1 teaspoon vanilla

Cream together. For flavorings, add the following to the base and whip until smooth. (Don't tell your children that the frosting is nutritious or they'll decide it's yucky before trying it.) Use on breads and muffins, as well as cookies and cakes.

Fruity Frosting

2 to 3 tablespoons fruit juice
1 cup non-fat dry milk
grated orange or lemon rind or
     chopped raisins or dates

Variation: You may substitute peanut butter for the butter or margarine in the base and add whatever else appeals to your family. Be sure to include the dry milk.

Spice Frosting

2 to 3 tablespoons milk,
    buttermilk or yogurt
1 cup nonfat dry milk
dashes of cinnamon, nutmeg
    and allspice

Banana Frosting

Mash one banana and add to spice frosting.

Chocolate or Carob Frosting

2 to 3 tablespoons milk, yogurt
    or buttermilk
¼ cup cocoa powder or carob
    powder
⅔ cup non-fat dry milk

More Frostings

- Sprinkle sugar and cinnamon on a cake or cookies just as you would on toast.

- Melt half a 6-ounce package of chocolate chips and half a cup of peanut butter and spread over cookies or bars.

- Spread honey on cookies to make a good "glue" for adding decors, coconut and other decorations.

- Dust confectioner's sugar on a cake or bar recipe for a completed look.

- Mix 1 tablespoon thawed orange juice concentrate with 1 cup powdered sugar to make a "dribble" frosting.

Snacks

Snacking is a way of life in most American households. It need not be a dirty word—nor need it be junk! Fruits and vegetables are the most obvious snack foods, plus most of the finger foods listed in the previous chapter. Junky snacks push the nutritious foods out of our diet, contribute to tooth decay and add pounds. But nutritious snacks should be considered part of your child's overall nutrition for the day.

We snack on what is handy. Having wholesome snacks on hand—bought or made—is part of our job.

Crackers are lower in sugar than cookies. Many are now available in reduced-salt versions. And don't forget lightly buttered whole grain toast.

Raisins (and other dried fruits) have recently fallen from favor in the dental community because they consist of sugars, albeit natural, that stick between teeth and promote tooth decay. Consider moving dried fruits from snacktime into the main mealtime.

Finger Jell-O

2 envelopes unflavored gelatin   1 package (6-ounce) or
2½ cups water   2 packages (3-ounce) Jell-O

It disappears before your very eyes! Dissolve unflavored gelatin in one cup of cold water. Set aside. In a saucepan, bring 1 cup of water to a boil and add Jell-O. Bring to a boil and remove from heat. Add gelatin mixture. Stir and add ½ cup cold water. Pour into a lightly greased pan and refrigerate until firm (about 2 hours). Cut into squares (or use a cookie cutter) and store in an airtight container in the refrigerator.

Or avoid using commercial Jell-O altogether by combining 3 envelopes of unflavored gelatin with one 12-ounce can of frozen juice concentrate and 12 ounces of water. Soften the gelatin in the thawed juice and bring the water to a boil. Add the juice/gelatin mixture to the boiling water and stir until gelatin dissolves. If the juice needs extra sweetening, add it here. Follow directions for chilling as in above recipe.

Apples in Hand

Peel (optional) and core a whole apple. Mix peanut butter with one of the following: raisins, wheat germ or granola. Stuff this mixture into the hole of the cored apple. Slice in half to serve. Or stick the apple half on a popsicle stick. It's both novel and neat that way.

Stuffed Celery

Stuff celery sticks with cream cheese or peanut butter. Raisins may be added on the top of the spread.

Depending on the age and chewing ability of the child, you may want to remove the strands from the celery.

Grinder Snacks

Grind figs, dates and raisins in equal amounts. (Nutmeats optional.) Add a small amount of lemon juice to a cup of graham cracker crumbs. Make small balls out of your ground mixture and roll in crumbs for coating. (Your baby food grinder can come in handy here.)

Peanut Butter Balls

½ cup peanut butter
3½ tablespoons non-fat dry
   milk
a bit of honey

Optional: raisins, nuts, coconut, wheat germ,
   sunflower seeds and
   brown sugar

Combine ingredients, roll into balls and store in refrigerator.

Goodie Balls

½ cup peanut butter
½ cup honey
½ cup instant cocoa or carob
   powder

1 cup peanuts or soy nuts
½ cup sunflower seeds
1 cup toasted wheat germ

Combine ingredients. Roll into balls and roll in coconut. Refrigerate if using a refrigerated brand of peanut butter, which is
preferable.

Chocolate/Peanut Butter Sticks

8 ounces semi-sweet
   chocolate
6 tablespoons peanut butter

1 teaspoon vanilla
1 cup toasted wheat germ

Melt chocolate and blend with peanut butter and vanilla. Stir in
wheat germ. Press into a buttered 8-inch square pan and chill until
firm. Cut into bars and store in a container in the refrigerator.

Uncandy Bars

1 loaf of bread (white, whole
   wheat or other)
1 package peanuts, chopped
1 cup peanut butter

peanut oil
¼ cup toasted wheat germ
   (optional)

Trim the crust from the bread. Cut bread slices in half. Put the
bread and the crusts on a cookie sheet overnight in the oven until
dry or place in a 150° oven for ½ hour or until dry. Put the dried
crusts only in a blender until finely crumbed. Combine crumbs
with chopped nuts. Add wheat germ, if desired. Thin the peanut

butter with oil. Spread or dip the bread slices in the peanut butter, then roll them in the nut/crumb mixture. Dry them on a cookie sheet. Store in an airtight container. No need to refrigerate if you are using shelf-stable peanut butter.

Variation: If candy isn't candy to you without chocolate, add 1 tablespoon instant cocoa to the thinned peanut butter.

Cheesy Wheats

4 cups spoon-size shredded
    wheat
½ cup margarine
1 cup cheese, shredded

In a large saucepan, melt margarine. Add cheese. When the cheese begins to melt, add shredded wheat. Toss to coat well. Refrigerate if not to be eaten within an hour or two. (This recipe can be easily adapted for a microwave oven.)

Cereal Sticks

½ cup butter or margarine
1 cup sugar
2 eggs
1 teaspoon vanilla
2½ cups flour (white, whole
    wheat or a combination)

¼ teaspoon baking soda
½ cup plus of cereal (such as
    Grape-Nuts, granola or
    wheat germ)

Blend the first six ingredients plus ¼ cup of the cereal together. If the dough is too soft, add more flour. Roll a small piece of dough into a stick and then roll the stick in the extra cereal to coat. (Employ anyone in your family who's experienced with playdough.) Place on a lightly greased cookie sheet and bake at 400° for 8 minutes or until slightly browned.

Oatmeal Bars

2 cups oatmeal, uncooked
¾ cup brown sugar

½ cup butter or margarine
dash of baking soda

Boil sugar, shortening and baking soda. Add oatmeal. Blend. Spread mixture in a well-greased 8-inch square pan and bake at 350° for 10 minutes. Cut into bars while warm.

Super Cookies

1½ cup oatmeal, uncooked (or
    Swiss Familia)
½ cup non-fat dry milk (or
    Tiger's Milk)
½ cup wheat germ

¾ cup sugar (or ½ cup honey)
1 teaspoon cinnamon
⅓ teaspoon cloves
½ cup oil or butter, melted
2 eggs, beaten

Mix dry ingredients. Add melted butter and beaten eggs. Spoon onto greased baking sheet. Bake at 350° for 12-15 minutes. ("Uncooked" oatmeal is also known as "rolled oats" or "old fashioned"—not the instant kind.)

Bite-of-Apple Cookies

½ cup margarine
1 cup brown sugar
2 eggs
1½ cups flour
½ cup oatmeal, uncooked

2 teaspoons baking soda
½ teaspoon cinnamon
¾ cup wheat germ
1 cup apples, peeled, cored
    and finely chopped

Cream shortening, sugar and eggs. Mix dry ingredients and combine with creamed mixture. Add apples. Drop spoonfuls onto a greased cookie sheet. Bake at 350° for 10-15 minutes.

Nutritious Brownies

¼ cup vegetable oil
1 tablespoon molasses
1 cup brown sugar
2 teaspoons vanilla
2 eggs
½ cup pecans or walnuts,
    broken

1 cup wheat germ
⅔ cup non-fat dry milk
½ teaspoon baking powder
¼ cup dry cocoa or 2 squares
    unsweetened baking
    chocolate

Mix together the first seven ingredients. (If using squares of chocolate, melt in a double boiler and add here.) Sift the dry milk, baking powder and cocoa through a sieve into the other ingredients and stir well. Spread in a heavily greased 8-inch square pan and bake at 350° for approximately 30 minutes. Turn out of pan immediately and cut into bars while still warm.

Fruit Roll

Use apples, peaches, pears, nectarines or canned pumpkin to make this yummy dried "candy." The fruit can be the "too-hard-to-eat" variety or the "too-ripe-and-the-last-piece" variety. It may even be well-drained, canned fruit. Mash or puree the fruit. Two methods work well:

Blender method: Peel and core fruit, blend until smooth, then cook 5 minutes in a saucepan over moderate heat.

Freeze-defrost method: In advance, peel and core fruit, wrap and freeze. Remove from freezer an hour before using so fruit can begin to defrost. Cook in a saucepan, mashing with a fork as you go, for 5-10 minutes. If the fruit is very watery, drain.

While cooking, add 1 teaspoon honey for each piece of fruit you are using. (Cook the different fruits separately, though you can cook one piece or a dozen of the same type at once.)

Lay out clear plastic wrap (or cut open small plastic bags) on cookie sheet or broiling tray. Use one piece of plastic for each piece of fruit you have cooked. Spoon mixture onto the wrap, staying away from its edge. Spread as thin as possible. Spread another piece of plastic wrap over the mixture and press down with a wide spatula to make evenly thin. Remove this top sheet of plastic before drying.

Turn oven to its lowest possible heat or just use the pilot light. Place tray in the oven and leave overnight (6-8 hours). The plastic wrap will not melt! If the fruit is dry by breakfast, remove from the oven. (If not, wait a while longer.) Roll up the plastic wrap (with the dried fruit) as if it were a jelly roll.

Then peel and eat!

The rolls will last several months this way—if your children don't discover them, that is. If you don't understand how this should look, stop in at a health food store and ask to look at their fruit rolls. And notice the price!

Variation: Core and peel an apple. Slice it into thin rings and dry as for fruit roll.

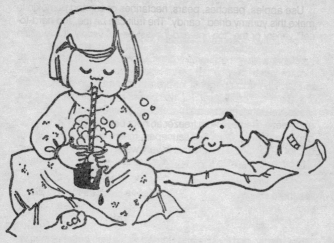

Pizza for Breakfast?

It's 7:45 in the morning. Your husband needs to leave for work by 8:15 and he's in the kitchen frying some eggs. You're giving milk to your three-month-old and your three-year-old, Chris, doesn't want any old fried eggs. He'd rather have leftover pizza for breakfast. Dad says, "No, pizza isn't breakfast food. Here's a nice piece of toast with jelly." You finish feeding and changing baby, give Chris some cold cereal with milk and sugar, plus a glass of orange juice, and then relax with a cup of coffee or tea. You guess you'll have something to eat around 10 a.m. Sound familiar?

No one wants to be creative at 7 a.m., but breakfast is a very important meal. And it's important for you to be as good a model as possible for your kids in this area as well as in other aspects of your life. People who skip breakfast are more likely to eat between meals and often consume more calories in a day than people who eat breakfast. If your child sees you eat a well-balanced breakfast, maybe he or she will develop good eating habits too.

Part of the problem stems from our stereotyped ideas of breakfast food, as just illustrated. Maybe now is the time to change our stereotypes about mealtime menus. A peanut butter sandwich, a hunk of cheese and whole wheat toast, or a container of yogurt are perfectly acceptable breakfast foods.

Leftovers have traditionally been served at lunch and dinner. Just for variation, why not serve leftover pizza, hamburger, casseroles, chops or spaghetti for breakfast? And save eggs, cereal or something "breakfasty" for the noon or evening meal. In a lot of cases, you don't even have to warm up the leftovers!

Breakfast Pizza

In case you have leftover spaghetti sauce, here's a good way to use it up!

spaghetti sauce
english muffins
butter or margarine

cheese (such as mozzarella, cheddar, American or Colby)

Split muffin and toast lightly. Spread with a little butter or margarine and top with 1 to 2 tablespoons spaghetti sauce. You may add bacon bits, mushrooms or anything else you want. Then lay a couple of slices of cheese on the top. Heat muffin pizza under the broiler until the cheese is gooey (3-5 minutes).

Other nontraditional possibilities for breakfast:

Grilled (or ungrilled) cheese sandwiches
Cottage cheese
Soup and cheese
Eggnog drinks (see page 15)

The following recipes are aimed, to a great extent, toward making breakfast enjoyable and nutritious, not only for your kids, but for your entire family.

Eggs

Eggs are a traditional part of the breakfast scene; some kids really go for them and others don't. Eggs are also good dinner fare. Here are a few ideas that may not convert the egg-haters, but that might lure the "not-so-crazy-about-eggs" bunch!

Bull's Eye

1 egg
1 slice bread
margarine or butter

Use a 2-inch round cookie cutter to cut out the center of the bread. Spread margarine generously on both sides of the bread. Brown one side of the bread in a moderately hot, greased frying pan and then turn over. Crack the egg into the hole in the bread and cook until the white is set. You may need to cover the pan to help the egg white set quickly. Lift out carefully and serve.

You may wish to use a cookie cutter shaped as a heart for Valentine's day, a bunny for Easter and a bell at Christmas.

Peanut Butter Custard

1⅓ cups milk
⅓ cup non-fat dry milk
⅓ cup peanut butter

2 eggs, beaten
3 tablespoons honey

Warm the liquid milk; stir in dry milk and blend with peanut butter until smooth. Mix in the eggs and honey and pour into greased custard cups. Set the cups in a pan of hot water (water should come up to the same level as the custard). Bake at 325° for 30 minutes or until a knife inserted in the center comes out clean. Refrigerate and serve cold.

Egg Posies

1 hard-boiled egg
1 slice bread, toasted and
    buttered
jelly

If you happen to have a special tool for slicing hard-boiled eggs into uniform rounds, your three-year-old can probably perform this job for you. If you don't have this gadget, slice the eggs the short way with a serrated knife into ¼-inch slices. Arrange the slices at the top of a medium-size plate so that they overlap and form a flower. Add a dab of jelly in the center. To make the leaves and stem, cut the slice of buttered toast into two triangles and one long strip. Arrange as shown. Voila!

Hint: If you have trouble with hard-boiled eggs cracking and whites coming out while cooking, try this method. Place eggs in deep kettle. Add cold water to 1 inch higher than the tops of the eggs. Heat to simmering (190°). Cover pan, remove from the burner and let set in the hot water for 20-25 minutes (depending on egg size). Run cold water over eggs as usual and peel.

Humpty Dumpty's Reprieve

Scrambled eggs are generally acceptable to the under-five generation. Here are a few suggestions to add a little spice and variety to this old favorite. Add:

- A sprinkling of wheat germ.
- Crisp bacon bits, artificial bacon bits, leftover meats or cooked vegetables.
- Cottage cheese or any grated cheese.
- Drained canned corn (saute corn in fat and then add eggs).
- Sauteed onion, celery and/or green pepper.
- Seasoned salad croutons.

Bread Omelet

2 tablespoons bread crumbs   ½ teaspoon butter or
2 tablespoons milk   margarine
1 egg, separated

Mix the bread crumbs and milk. Soak for 15 minutes or overnight in a covered bowl in the refrigerator. In another bowl, beat the egg yolk well. In a third bowl, beat the egg white until stiff but not dry. Add the yolk to the bread crumb mixture and fold in the beaten whites. Cook in a small or medium-size, greased frying pan until mixture is set on the top and browned on the bottom. Remove and serve with butter, jelly or honey. Optional additions are bacon bits and/or pieces of leftover meat.

Breakfast Fruit Combinations

Vitamin C is an important part of breakfast, but again it need not always be served in the traditional orange juice. Consider some of these combinations:

- Apricots and cottage cheese.
- Cantaloupe slices.
- Grapes, apples and other fruit with cheese chunks.
- Mandarin oranges with sour cream or yogurt.
- Orange slices cut into circles.
- Sliced peaches and blueberries.
- Strawberries and pineapple chunks.

When serving an orange, roll it on the counter prior to cutting it to get more juice.

Orange juice is best when freshly squeezed, but frozen is cheaper. Make sure orange juice cans say "juice," not "drink," and also "no sugar added."

From the Griddle

Pancakes and waffles are lots of fun for the whole family. There are prepared mixes for both, plus frozen waffles, which are real timesavers. If you do have the time, here are some basic recipes that just could become a traditional part of your weekend breakfasts.

Buttermilk Beauties

1 cup flour (white, whole wheat or a combination)	1 egg
1 teaspoon baking powder	1 cup buttermilk (or plain yogurt, plus sweet milk or
½ teaspoon baking soda	water to make 1 cup
1 tablespoon shortening, melted, or oil	liquid)

Mix dry ingredients. Add milk and shortening to egg and mix. Combine the two mixtures until they are just moistened. Bake on a hot griddle, browning both sides.

Great Groovy Griddle Cakes

1½ cups flour (white, whole
    wheat or a combination)
1¾ teaspoons baking powder
3 tablespoons sugar or honey

2 eggs
3 tablespoons shortening,
    melted, or vegetable oil
1 or 1¼ cups milk

Combine dry ingredients in a large bowl. Beat eggs; add sugar, shortening and milk. Add wet ingredients to the dry ingredients and mix until barely moistened. Ignore the lumps. Set covered mixture in a cool, dry place as long as possible (even overnight, if possible). Bake on a lightly greased griddle or frying pan. When bubbles appear on upper surface of the cakes, turn and brown on second side.

Cottage Cheese Pancakes

3 eggs
1 cup cottage cheese
2 tablespoons salad oil or
    butter, melted

2 tablespoons flour or
    cornmeal

With a small mixer (or a blender) beat eggs. Add cottage cheese and mix until fairly smooth. Add shortening and flour. Make cakes on the "smallish" side. Bake as usual for pancakes.

Personalized Pancakes

For the child who is starting to learn letters and numbers, what fun it is to have a stack of pancakes with initials or age on the top of each cake. Offer this on birthday morning, or to celebrate a newly learned letter or number. Here's how you do it!

Dip a teaspoon into pancake batter and let excess drip off. With remaining batter, draw the letter or number *backwards* on the hot, greased pan or griddle. (You might need to practice your mirror-writing on paper.)

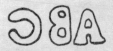

When the underside is lightly browned, pour a spoonful of regular batter *over* the letter or number so that the pancake will completely surround it. Bake until bubbles appear; then turn and brown second side. The letter or number will appear darker on the finished pancake.

Or try Animal Pancakes, like this:

Crumpets

"Tea and crumpets" is an expression that crops up fairly regularly in English novels and films. This recipe is one of many varieties.

3 cups flour (white, whole wheat or a combination)
1 tablespoon baking powder
2 tablespoons sugar or honey

2 tablespoons butter or margarine
1 egg
1½ to 1¾ cups milk

Mix flour, baking powder and sugar. Cut in shortening until mixture is like bread crumbs. Beat egg with milk. Combine wet and dry ingredients and stir just enough to moisten. (The batter should be thick, but if it doesn't spread when dropped on griddle, add some more milk.) Drop batter by tablespoons onto hot, greased griddle. Bake as usual for pancakes.

Thin any leftover batter with a bit more milk to make larger cakes. Use instead of bread for a sandwich.

Wonderful Waffles

2 cups flour (white, whole wheat or a combination)
2 teaspoons baking powder
2 tablespoons sugar or honey

2 eggs, separated
2 cups milk
4 to 6 tablespoons shortening, melted, or oil

Sift dry ingredients twice. (If using whole wheat flour, add back particles that would not go through.) Beat egg yolks, then mix with shortening and honey (if you're using it) and milk. Mix dry and liquid ingredients just enough to blend them. Beat egg whites until stiff and fold into batter. Bake according to manufacturer's instructions for your waffle iron.

Make additional waffles from your leftover batter and freeze them for later use. All you need to do is pop them in a toaster prior to eating. Or if you're super-organized, make the whole batch ahead and freeze them for a series of yummy, fast breakfasts.

Variations on the pancake and waffle theme. To the batter add:

- Fresh or frozen drained berries and a little extra sweetening. (If possible let batter sit ½ hour when adding fresh berries.)

- Chopped nut meats (again let sit ½ hour if possible).

- Grated orange rind.

- Finely diced ham or bacon bits.

- Non-fat dry milk.

- Or replace part of the flour called for with soy flour, wheat germ, brewer's yeast or corn meal for more nutritional value.

- Divide batter and add a few drops of food coloring to each batch so you can offer a colored collection on a platter.

- For waffles—pour batter and then place a piece of uncooked bacon on batter in each section of the iron. Close iron and bake as usual.

Suggested toppings for pancakes and waffles:

- Cinnamon mixed with sugar or honey.

- Peanut butter and jelly or honey.

- Ice cream topped with wheat germ.

- Sweetened applesauce mixed with sour cream or yogurt.

- Canned or fresh fruits such as peaches, berries or bananas (roll pancakes around any of the above fruits, secure with a toothpick and serve the "logs" with syrup and butter).

- The traditional maple syrup or honey and butter.

French Toast

French toast is a good way to combine eggs, milk and bread. If you are going to use homemade whole grain bread for this purpose, be very careful as you lift the bread slices from the egg-milk mixture into the pan. They are usually more fragile than white bread after being soaked and can break easily.

Here are two batter recipes:

1 egg		1 egg
⅓ cup milk	Or	4 teaspoons flour
⅛ teaspoon vanilla		⅓ cup milk

For both recipes, beat eggs lightly and add next two ingredients. Dip bread into the mixture. Fry in a well-greased pan over fairly high heat, browning well on both sides. Or on a cold morning, preheat the oven to 500° and bake the dipped bread on a greased pan, turning after the tops brown. Makes approximately 3 slices each.

Serve with any of the suggested toppings for pancakes and waffles.

French Toast Waffles

1 egg, beaten	½ teaspoon cinnamon
¼ cup milk	bread slices
2 tablespoons shortening, melted, or salad oil	1 to 2 tablespoons sugar or honey (optional)

Combine all ingredients except the bread and mix well. Cut the bread to fit the waffle iron. Dip bread into the batter and bake on a hot, greased iron until well browned. (It may be necessary to hold the top of the iron down for a little while since the bread has more height than batter alone.)

French Pancakes

1 slice bread (preferably whole wheat)	¼ teaspoon vanilla or maple extract
1 egg	1 tablespoon milk

Combine the above ingredients in a blender. Whir until smooth. Cook as for pancakes.

Cereals

Cereal is one of the first foods we give our children and it generally continues in the diet as a breakfast staple. Historically, cereal began as a nourishing whole grain breakfast food. Processing has changed the food value, but not the tradition. Much has been published about the lack of nutritional value in highly processed dry cereals on the market. Although a child does get some vitamins and minerals, as the cereal manufacturers state, most of the nutritional value comes from the accompanying serving of milk. Some manufacturers spray their cereals with additional vitamins, giving you virtual vitamin pellets, which are not a good substitute for a whole grain or unprocessed cereal. If you buy fortified breakfast cereals, you may be paying dearly for a few cents' worth of vitamins. According to the Center for Science in the Public Interest in Washington, D.C., Total, for instance, is the same product as Wheaties, except for the sprayed-on vitamins. Note the difference in the prices of these products. Read your cereal labels!

Also, you will find that many of today's popular cereals are mainly sugar—a poor way to start off the day. It is cheaper and more nutritious to add a teaspoon of sugar or artificial sweetener to a non-sweetened cereal. Avoid cereals that are sugar-frosted, honey-coated or chocolate-flavored.

Some cereals that contain *no* sugars are: Cream of Wheat (farina), Quaker Oats, Shredded Wheat, Nutri-Grain, Kretschmer Wheat Germ and Wheatena. The sugar in many of the dry cereals tends to encourage children to expect sweets along with the main part of breakfast as well as other meals.

Hot Cereal

Many kinds of hot cooked cereals are on the market, such as Malt-O-Meal, Roman Meal, Cream of Wheat, Cream of Rice, Oatmeal (old-fashioned variety) and others. These can be pepped up to look and taste better in any of the following ways:

- Hide one or two chocolate chips in a bowl of cereal for a bit of adventure.
- Add a heaping teaspoon of creamy peanut butter.

- Add raisins, dates, drained canned fruit, frozen fruit and especially fresh fruit.

- Use any of the above to create a design on the bowl of cereal, such as a face with raisins for eyes and nose, and peach slices for mouth and ears. Draw a spiral design of jelly, or a lacy design a la Jackson Pollack, made by drizzling some molasses from a spoon. Use your imagination!

- Add wheat germ, cooked soy grits, and/or non-fat dry milk.

Homemade Hot Rice Cereal

Grind several cups of raw brown rice to a fine powder in a blender. Store in a tightly covered container. To prepare:

½ cup rice powder
2 cups milk
dash of salt

In a small saucepan, bring milk and salt just to boiling point. Add the rice powder, stirring constantly. Lower heat, cover pan and simmer for 8-10 minutes. Serve with butter or margarine, honey, molasses, wheat germ, fruit or whatever your family likes. It has a nutty taste.

Corn-off-the-Cob Hot Cereal

¼ cup yellow cornmeal	2 teaspoons wheat germ
¼ cup cold water	(optional)
¾ cup boiling water	¼ cup non-fat dry milk
	(optional)

Mix together cornmeal, cold water and wheat germ (if you're using it). Bring the ¾ cup water to a boil and add the cornmeal mixture and the dry milk (if you're using it). Stirring constantly, bring to a boil and let boil about 2 minutes. Cool and serve with any of the following: butter, margarine, cottage cheese, sour cream, yogurt, jam, honey, brown sugar, maple syrup, raisins or chopped dates.

Millet

1 cup whole millet
4 cups water

Put cereal and water in the top of a double boiler and place over direct heat. Boil for 5 minutes. Then put top of boiler over the bottom pot which contains more water. Simmer 30-45 minutes, then turn off heat and let it steam for a while longer.

Cold Cereal

One idea for a nutritious and easy bowl of cereal is to crumble a whole grain muffin in a bowl. Pour milk over it, add fruit, nuts or sweetener and you have an instant breakfast.

One popular natural cold cereal on the shelves these days is granola, which is being marketed under a variety of names. Check the list of ingredients carefully, since most granolas have a high sugar content.

Better yet, try making your own granola. It's easy, cheaper and the proportions of ingredients can be changed around to fit your family's preference. It can also be ground in a blender and served with milk to babies and young children who would choke on the unground cereal. Another way to soften granola is to let it sit in a bowl of milk overnight in the refrigerator.

Granola

4 cups oatmeal, uncooked
1½ cups wheat germ (raw or
    toasted)
1 cup coconut, grated
¼ cup non-fat dry milk
1 to 2 tablespoons cinnamon
1 tablespoon brown sugar

⅓ cup vegetable oil
½ cup honey
1 tablespoon vanilla
½ cup sesame seeds
    (optional)
½ cup raw nuts, seeds or rais-
    ins (optional)

In a large bowl, mix dry ingredients. Combine oil, honey and vanilla in a saucepan and warm. Add these to the dry ingredients and stir until all the particles are coated. (Hand mixing works well here.) Spread this mixture in a long, low pan or rimmed baking sheet that has been greased. Bake at *either* 250° for an hour *or* 300° for half an hour, depending on your schedule. Turn with a spatula from time to time. When finished toasting, add dried fruits, such as raisins. Cool and store in an airtight container.

Wheat Germ

Raw wheat germ has greater nutritional value than the toasted kind, but is less palatable. So it is probably preferable to use the toasted kind as a breakfast cereal and be assured your kids will like it. Several brands are available, some with additions such as honey and cinnamon. Serve any of these as regular cereal with milk without making a big to-do about it and see what reaction your kids have. Or, if you use raw wheat germ in your cooking, and want to toast your own, here's one way to do it:

4 cups raw wheat germ
    (always keep in
    refrigerator)
½ cup honey, approximately
    (warmed a bit)

Mix thoroughly and spread mixture on a well-greased baking sheet. Bake at 300° for 10 minutes in bottom third of oven. Cool and store in airtight container in refrigerator.

Additional serving ideas:

- Sprinkle on peanut butter sandwiches.

- Mix with other sandwich fillings.

- Add to meat loaf (approximately ¼ cup).

- Toss a little in a green salad.

Rice Pudding

Usually eaten as a hearty dessert, rice pudding is a nice change-of-pace for breakfast while including milk, egg and a grain.

2 cups cooked rice (preferably
    brown rice)
2 cups milk
½ cup non-fat dry milk
¼ cup brown sugar
1 tablespoon butter or marga-
    rine, melted

2 eggs, well-beaten
½ lemon rind, grated
½ teaspoon vanilla
¼ cup raisins
bread crumbs or wheat germ

Mix all ingredients together except crumbs or wheat germ. Grease a 1-quart casserole dish (or individual custard cups) and sprinkle bottom with some crumbs or wheat germ. Pour in pudding mixture and sprinkle more crumbs on top. Bake at 350° for 20 minutes or until a knife inserted in the center comes out clean. (For children, this is best prepared in advance and served cold.)

Breakfast Cookies

Although you may not want to make a regular practice of it, nutritious cookies can be a fun and interesting breakfast, as well as a good snack or dessert. Many cookie recipes can be thinned with a little milk and baked in a square pan to make bars, so you have two versions of the same recipe.

Bacon 'n Egg Cookies

1¼ cup flour (white or whole wheat)
⅔ cup brown sugar
½ cup Grape-Nuts cereal
½ pound bacon, cooked crisp and crumbled (or ½ cup artificial bacon bits)

½ cup shortening, melted
1 egg, beaten
2 tablespoons frozen orange juice concentrate, undiluted
1 tablespoon orange peel, grated

Mix flour, sugar, Grape-Nuts and bacon. Add remaining ingredients and blend well. Drop by tablespoonfuls onto a greased cookie sheet (ungreased if real bacon is used) and bake at 350° for 10-12 minutes or until cookies are light brown.

Banana Oatmeal Cookies

¾ cup shortening
1 cup brown sugar
1 egg, beaten
1½ cups flour (white, whole wheat or a combination)
½ teaspoon baking soda
1 teaspoon cinnamon

¼ teaspoon nutmeg
1 cup mashed banana
1¾ cups oatmeal, uncooked
Optional: raisins, nuts, wheat germ, sunflower seeds, grated orange peel

Cream shortening with sugar, add the egg and mix well. Mix flour, baking soda, cinnamon and nutmeg together and add to creamed mixture. Blend until smooth. Add mashed banana and oatmeal next. Blend. Drop by teaspoonfuls onto a greased cookie sheet and bake at 400° for 12-15 minutes.

Oatmeal Overnight Cookies

4 cups oatmeal, uncooked
2 cups brown sugar
1 cup bland oil
2 eggs, beaten

1 teaspoon flavoring (vanilla or almond)
¼ cup wheat germ (optional)

In the evening, combine oatmeal, brown sugar and oil. The next morning, add eggs, flavoring and wheat germ (if desired). Mix well. Drop by spoonfuls onto a greased cookie sheet and bake at 300° for 12-15 minutes. Watch cookies carefully. Remove from sheet while still warm or you may never get them off.

Granola Breakfast Bars

2 cups granola
2 eggs, beaten
dash of vanilla (optional)

Combine the granola and eggs in a greased 8-inch square pan. Bake at 350° for 15 minutes. Cut into 8 bars. When serving spread with jam, honey or peanut butter.

Wheels of Steel

½ cup butter or margarine
½ cup peanut butter
1 cup brown sugar, packed
1 egg, beaten
1 teaspoon vanilla
¾ cup whole wheat flour
1 cup oatmeal, uncooked
¼ cup wheat germ, raw or toasted

½ cup non-fat dry milk
¼ teaspoon baking powder
¼ teaspoon baking soda
3 tablespoons liquid milk
1 cup raisins
sesame seeds (optional)

Cream shortening until smooth. Add peanut butter, sugar, egg and vanilla. Beat well. In a separate bowl, combine flour, wheat germ, dry milk, baking powder and baking soda. Add the dry ingredients to the wet and stir well. Add liquid milk, oatmeal and raisins. Blend. On a greased cookie sheet, spread a heaping spoonful of dough into a circle. The cookies spread as they bake, so leave an inch or more between them. Sprinkle tops with sesame seeds and press into dough. Bake at 375° for 10-12 minutes. Allow cookies to cool before removing—they are very fragile while warm.

Cereal Balls

1 cup ground-in-a-blender
    cereal (such as shredded
    wheat, granola, wheat
    germ)

1 tablespoon honey
milk, as much as needed
1 tablespoon peanut butter
    (optional)

After grinding cereal, add honey and peanut butter. Blend. Add milk until mixture can be rolled into balls. Refrigerate in a covered container.

Variations:

- Roll into logs; roll logs in coconut or wheat germ.

- Add non-fat dry milk and brown sugar, and eliminate peanut butter, liquid milk and honey. Store in a plastic bag for a convenient treat when traveling. Just add water as needed for a breakfast food or snack.

Creamy Balls

Combine chopped nuts and cream cheese. Roll into balls and serve.

Quick Breads

If the quick breads in your repertoire of family favorites call for white flour, try substituting whole wheat flour. Or use the Cornell Triple-Rich Formula (see page 62) with the flour you're using. When substituting whole grain flour for white, use more baking powder since whole grains require a bit more help in rising.

Peanut Butter Bread

2 cups flour (white, whole
    wheat or a combination)
4 teaspoons baking powder

¼ cup sugar or honey
1¼ cups milk
⅔ cup peanut butter

Lightly mix dry ingredients in a large bowl. If using honey, cream it with the peanut butter in a separate bowl. Heat the milk until lukewarm, then add the peanut butter and blend well. Add the wet and dry ingredients and beat thoroughly. Pour into a greased loaf pan and bake at 350° for 45-50 minutes. When the bread is cold, make thin slices and spread with honey or jam. This slices best if baked a day in advance and refrigerated after cooking.

Breakfast Banana Nut Bread

¼ cup butter or margarine
½ cup brown sugar
1 egg, beaten
1 cup bran cereal or oatmeal, uncooked
4 to 5 ripe bananas (about 1½ cups), mashed

1 teaspoon vanilla
1½ cups flour (white, whole wheat or a combination)
2 teaspoons baking powder
½ teaspoon baking soda
½ cup nuts, chopped

Cream shortening and sugar until light. Add egg and mix well. Stir in cereal, bananas and vanilla. Combine the remaining ingredients in a bowl and add to the first mixture, stirring just long enough to moisten the flour. Grease and flour a loaf pan; pour in batter. Bake at 350° for 1 hour or until bread tests done.

Hint: What to do with that leftover, ripe banana? Mash it, add a bit of lemon juice or Fruit Fresh and freeze until you make banana bread. If chopped nuts aren't yet appropriate for your child, whirl them in a blender before adding to batter.

Ready Bran Muffins

2 cups boiling water
6 cups 100-percent bran cereal
1 cup shortening (butter, Crisco or margarine)
2 cups sugar or 1⅔ cups honey

4 eggs, beaten
1 quart buttermilk
5 cups flour (white, whole wheat or a combination)
5 teaspoons baking soda

Preheat oven to 375°. Pour boiling water over 2 cups of the cereal and set aside. Cream shortening with sugar or honey and add the eggs, buttermilk and the moistened bran cereal, and mix. Fold in the remaining dry ingredients. Fill greased muffin tins ¾-full and bake 20-25 minutes. Or fill a loaf pan ½-full and bake at 350° until done. Batter can be stored in quart jars in the refrigerator for up to six weeks.

Hint: The proportions called for in this recipe make several quarts of batter. If it's too much, cut the recipe in half, give some to a neighbor, or store in the freezer.

Optional additions: blueberries, raisins, coconut, peanuts, chopped fresh apples, chopped dates, nuts, a cube of cheese.

Whole Wheat Muffins

1 cup whole wheat flour
¾ cup white flour
¼ cup sugar or honey
4 teaspoons baking powder

1 egg
1 cup milk
¼ cup salad oil

Mix dry ingredients. In a separate bowl, beat egg slightly and stir in milk and oil. Add wet ingredients to dry ingredients and stir until just moistened. Batter will be lumpy. Fill greased muffin tins ⅔-full and bake at 400° for 20-25 minutes. Remove muffins from tins immediately after baking.

Orange Muffins

1 slice bread (preferably whole grain)
1 egg
⅓ cup non-fat dry milk

½ teaspoon baking soda
1 orange, peeled and cut up
1 tablespoon water
4 teaspoons honey or sugar

Put the bread in a bowl and pull apart with a fork. Mix remaining ingredients together and combine with the bread. Spoon into greased muffin cups until ⅔-full, and bake at 350° for 30 minutes.

Quickie Turnovers

1 can (8 ounce) refrigerated crescent rolls

Filling:

½ cup honey
1 tablespoon sunflower seeds

1 tablespoon raisins
¼ cup blueberries

Combine all the filling ingredients. Unroll the crescent rolls and place a spoonful of the filling mixture in the middle of each triangle of dough. Moisten the edges of the dough. Following the diagram on the package, fold point A over to point C. Press edges firmly together. Place on a greased cookie sheet and bake at 375° for 10-12 minutes.

Filling variations:

Peanut butter		Honey
Jelly		Granola
Non-fat dry milk	Or	Apple slices
Raisins		Cinnamon and nuts

Bread

The art of baking bread is coming back into its own in this country. If you've never tried it, why not start now? The aroma of yeast bread baking is a delight, one to which you and your family could take a real liking. Being home with small children gives you the type of time slots needed for making bread: 5 to 10 minutes of concentrated work, spread over several hours.

Batter breads are somewhat simpler than breads that must be kneaded, so try a batter recipe if you are a new bread baker.

If baking bread just isn't "your thing," consider using frozen bread dough from your grocer's freezer section. You merely let it thaw and rise, then bake. Most frozen doughs don't contain all those extra ingredients that make bread shelf-stable, but the bread tastes and smells so good that it disappears very quickly. The major disadvantage of this bread is that it is difficult to slice thin.

You have probably noticed in this book that when flour is called for the recipe generally gives you a choice of white, whole wheat, or a mixture of the two. Here is what the authors of *The Joy of Cooking* have to say about bleached enriched white flour:

"After the removal of the outer coats and germ, our flours may be enriched, but the term is misleading. Enriched flours contain only four of the many ingredients known to have been removed from it in the milling."

You can give additional food value to white flour for cakes, cookies, muffins, and breads by using the simple method below, called the Cornell Triple-Rich Formula.

Cornell Triple-Rich Formula

1 tablespoon soy flour
1 tablespoon non-fat dry milk
1 teaspoon raw wheat germ

Place these ingredients in the bottom of your measuring cup before adding flour. Then add flour to make one cup. Do this for each cup of flour you use. Eventually you may want to add a little more of each enricher. Whole grain flours, too, benefit from this formula.

Bread-Making Procedures

In case you're wondering how to tell if the bread dough or batter has *doubled in bulk*, here's an easy way to find out. Press lightly with one or two fingers near the edge of the dough. If a small indentation remains, it has doubled. If not, the dough will spring back.

When bread is *browning too fast* (turning a light brown after only 10-15 minutes), cover the top lightly with a piece of aluminum foil.

If you've *never kneaded*, don't let that stop you. You'll improve with practice, so start experimenting now. Kneading is a process of folding the dough and pressing it down with the heel of your hand, over and over again, until the dough is smooth and elastic, not sticky. You may need to sprinkle flour on the dough and/or your working surface when you begin until the dough loses some of its stickiness.

If you need a *warm place to let your bread rise* where busy little fingers can't reach, place a baking pan filled with about an inch of hot water on the bottom of your oven. Put the bowl or pans of dough that are rising on the middle shelf. You may have to replace water every half hour or so with more warm water. And don't forget to remove the pan of water when you bake your bread!

Or heat your oven to 200° for 60 seconds. Turn off. Then put in bread for rising.

Basic Whole Wheat Bread

1 cup warm water (105°-115°)	⅓ cup honey
2 packages yeast	1½ tablespoons salt
1 tablespoon honey	5 cups whole wheat flour
2 cups milk	3 cups white flour
¼ cup butter, margarine or oil	¼ cup wheat germ (optional)

Dissolve yeast in warm water. Stir in 1 tablespoon honey. Set aside for 10 minutes. In a saucepan, combine milk, butter (or margarine or oil), honey and salt. Heat to lukewarm—do not scald. Pour warm milk mixture and dissolved yeast into a large mixing bowl. Add the whole wheat flour, one cup at a time, beating well after each addition. Be sure to use all the whole wheat flour. Add wheat germ, if desired.

Add enough white flour to make a soft, yet manageable, dough. Turn out on a lightly floured board and knead until smooth and elastic, approximately 8-10 minutes.

Place dough in a greased bowl, turning it to grease the top. Cover and let rise in a warm, draft-free place until dough has doubled in bulk. Punch down, divide in half and knead each half for about 30 seconds.

Shape into three loaves and place in greased loaf pans. Cover and let rise again until doubled in bulk, about 45 minutes.

Preheat oven to 400° and bake 40 minutes or until done.

Cinnamon Swirl Bread

Follow the above dough recipe but before shaping the dough, roll into three rectangles, about 6" x 16" each. Mix together 4 tablespoons brown sugar and 4 tablespoons cinnamon; sprinkle ¼ cup of this mixture over each rectangle. Beginning with the narrow side, roll up tightly into a loaf; seal ends and bottom by pinching dough together to make a seam. Place in the loaf pans and proceed as in the above recipe.

Refrigerator 100 Percent Whole Wheat Bread

This recipe is an especially good one if you have an outside job or are too busy during the day with the kids or whatever to make bread. Mix the dough in the evening, set it in the refrigerator and let it rise and bake the next evening. If the dough is to be refrigerated for only 3 hours, use lukewarm liquid; if it is to be left longer, cool liquid so dough will not rise too much. Dough may still require punching down a few times while it is in the refrigerator.

5 cups milk or water	¼ cup honey
2 packages dry yeast, dissolved in 1 cup warm water (105°-115°)	11 to 12 cups whole wheat flour (or a combination of 9 to 10 cups whole wheat and 1 to 2 cups soy flour)
½ cup shortening, melted, or oil	2 tablespoons salt
¼ cup molasses	

In a 6-quart pan or bowl, mix together the liquid, dissolved yeast, shortening, honey, molasses and salt. Add flour gradually, mixing well after each addition. (If using soy flour, add after at least 4 cups of whole wheat flour have been added.) This dough will be more moist than ordinary bread dough. Let dough rest in the bowl 10-15 minutes.

Turn dough out on a floured board and knead for about 10 minutes, adding as little extra flour as possible. Replace in the bowl, cover with foil or a dampened cloth and refrigerate immediately for 3-24 hours. Remove from the refrigerator, punch down and let stand 30-60 minutes at room temperature.

Divide into four equal portions, shape into loaves and place in four well-greased loaf pans (see note below). Lightly grease the tops of the loaves. Let rise in a warm, draft-free place until almost doubled in bulk. Preheat oven to 425°, place pans in oven, reduce heat to 325° and bake for 1 hour or until done. This dough makes excellent hamburger buns. Use ¼ to ⅓ cup of dough for each bun. Bake at 325° for 25-30 minutes or until done.

Hint: If your oven won't hold four pans at one time or you don't own four pans, remove only enough dough from the refrigerator as you can bake at one time. But be sure to take the rest out and use it within 24 hours.

Swiss Cheese Bread

This bread tastes very nearly like a grilled Swiss cheese sandwich when toasted. And its braided, glazed top makes it very pretty!

1½ cups milk
2 tablespoons sugar or honey
1 tablespoon salt
2 tablespoons butter, margarine or oil
2 cups grated Swiss cheese (8 ounces)

2 packages dry yeast
½ cup warm water (105°-115°)
5 cups white flour (approximately)
1 egg and poppy or sesame seeds (optional)

Preheat oven to 350°. Scald milk and combine with sugar or honey, salt, shortening and cheese in a large bowl. (Cheese will probably melt into a lump, but don't worry.) Let cool until lukewarm. Dissolve yeast in the warm water and add to the cooled milk mixture. Stir well. Gradually add flour, stirring well after each addition until a fairly stiff dough is formed.

Knead dough about 5-8 minutes. Place in a greased bowl, turning to grease top; let it rise in a warm, draft-free place until doubled in bulk.

Punch down and divide the dough into two equal portions. Roll each piece out into an 11" x 15" rectangle. Cut each rectangle into three equal strips (the long way), leaving the strips joined at one end.

Braid the strips loosely. Pinch the three ends together. Place each braided loaf in a well-greased pan. Cover and let rise until doubled. Bake 40-45 minutes.

Variation: Just before popping loaves in the oven, beat an egg with 1 tablespoon cool water and brush on tops of loaves. Sprinkle on seeds.

Triple-Rich Batter White Bread

A good choice for a new baker.

1 cup milk
3 tablespoons sugar or honey
1 tablespoon salt
2 tablespoons oil or shortening, melted

1 cup warm water (105°-115°)
2 packages dry yeast
4¼ cups white flour, unsifted
Cornell Triple-Rich Formula (page 62)

Scald milk; stir in sugar or honey, salt and shortening. Set aside to cool until lukewarm (105°-115°).

Add yeast to the warm water in a large bowl and stir until dissolved. Pour warm milk mixture into the yeast. Stir in the flour, one cup at a time, placing the soy flour, dry milk and wheat germ in the bottom of the measuring cup first. Beat with a long-handled spoon for about 2 minutes, or longer if using whole wheat flour.

Cover with a cloth and let rise in a warm, draft-free place until more than doubled in bulk (about 40 minutes). Stir batter down and beat vigorously for about 30 seconds.

Grease two loaf pans, 9" x 5" x 3". Divide batter evenly between them. Batter does not need to rise again. Preheat oven to 375° and bake for about 50 minutes.

Variations:

- Try using part or all whole wheat flour. Beat a minute or two longer than for white flour.

- Add 1 or more beaten eggs for a different texture.

Raisin 'n Egg Batter Bread

This bread has a rich, cake-like quality.

1 cup milk	2 packages dry yeast
½ cup sugar or honey	1 egg, beaten
1 teaspoon salt	4½ cups white flour
¼ cup shortening or vegetable oil	1 cup raisins
½ cup warm water (105°-115°)	Cornell Triple-Rich Formula (optional—see page 62)

Preheat oven to 350°. Scald milk. Stir in sugar, honey, salt and shortening. Let cool to lukewarm (105°-115°).

Add yeast to warm water in a large bowl and stir until dissolved. Pour the warm milk mixture into the yeast. Add the egg and then mix in 3 cups of the flour, beating well after each addition. After the third cup, beat until smooth. Stir in remaining flour to make a stiff batter.

Cover with a cloth and let rise in a warm, draft-free place until doubled in bulk (about one hour). Stir batter down and beat in raisins, distributing them as evenly as possible.

Grease two 1-quart casserole dishes or two loaf pans and divide the batter evenly between them. Batter does not need to rise again. Bake for 40-45 minutes or until done.

English Muffins

This is a good summer bread because you don't have to turn on the oven.

1 cup milk, scalded	1 package dry yeast
2 tablespoons sugar or honey	5 to 6 cups flour (white, whole
¼ cup butter, oil or margarine	wheat or a combination)
1 tablespoon salt	cornmeal
1 cup warm water (105°-115°)	

Place hot milk in a large bowl and add shortening, sugar (or honey) and salt. Let cool to lukewarm.

Dissolve yeast in the warm water and add to the cooled milk. Add 3 cups of flour and beat until smooth. Gradually add more flour, beating well after each addition until a soft dough is formed.

Turn out on a lightly floured board and knead until smooth and elastic (8-10 minutes), adding more flour as necessary. Place in a greased bowl, turning to grease the top. Cover and let rise in a warm, draft-free place until doubled in bulk (about 1 hour). Punch down and divide in half.

On a lightly floured board, roll the first half out to about ½-inch thick and cut as many circles of dough as you can with a muffin cutter (see hint). Gently remove to a cookie sheet that has been heavily sprinkled with corn meal. Sprinkle tops with corn meal, too.

Push scraps together, roll out and cut again. Continue until all the dough is used. Cover the muffins with a cloth and let rise until doubled.

To bake, heat a griddle or electric fry pan to moderately hot (about 300°) and grease lightly. Using a large spatula, move as many muffins as will fit (without touching) to the griddle. Bake until bottoms are browned (10-15 minutes). Then turn and bake other side.

To cut, insert tines of fork all the way around and pull apart with your fingers.

Hint: A 7-ounce tuna-type can with both ends removed is a perfect cutter for the muffins. But for fun, try cutting them with large, not-too-detailed cookie cutters. (Some won't keep their shape and some will.)

Bagels

1½ cups warm water (105°-
    115°)
1 package dry yeast
1 tablespoon salt
3 tablespoons sugar or honey

4 to 6 cups flour (white, whole
    wheat or a combination)
1 egg
poppy or sesame seeds
    (optional)

Preheat oven to 375°. In a large bowl, mix warm water with yeast and add salt and sugar (or honey). Cover bowl and let stand 5 minutes. Gradually add the flour until a soft-to-medium (but not stiff) dough is obtained.

Knead on a lightly floured board, 5-10 minutes until shiny and smooth. Add a little more flour as necessary for kneading. Place in a greased bowl, turning to grease the top. Cover and let rise in a warm, draft-free place until doubled, about 30 minutes. Punch down and knead lightly.

To shape into bagels, roll approximately ¼ cup dough into a strand about 7 inches long and pinch the ends firmly together. Place bagels fairly close together on a floured board or cookie sheet, cover and let rise again about 30 minutes in a warm place.

In the meantime, bring about 5 inches of water to boil in a fairly large, open kettle. Turn heat down so water is simmering. When bagels have risen, gently lift one at a time and drop into the simmering water. Turn them immediately and simmer for about 2 minutes, until puffy but not disintegrating. Several bagels may be in the water at one time, but do not crowd the pan. Remove the bagels to a towel-covered area to drain and cool while you are boiling the next batch. Place cooled bagels on greased baking sheet. They can be close together.

Beat the egg briefly with 1 tablespoon of cool water and brush mixture over the tops of the bagels. Sprinkle with poppy or sesame seeds, if desired. Bake for 30-40 minutes.

This procedure may look complicated at first, but once you get the knack, you can turn out a batch in 3 to 3½ hours, from start to finish. Makes 12-15 bagels.

Seasonal Recipes

Here are some seasonal ideas that are often more fun than nutritious, but worth trying on occasion. Many of the ideas here are sugary and should be served in moderation.

Summary

Summer means little hands constantly opening the refrigerator in search of things to quench thirst and hunger.

Yogurt Popsicles

1 carton plain yogurt
1 can (6 ounce) concentrated
    fruit juice, unsweetened
    (orange seems to be a
    favorite)

dash of vanilla and/or honey
    (optional)

Mix well and freeze in molds (3-ounce paper cups work well). For handles, insert wooden sticks or spoons when mixture is partially frozen.

Variation: Make single servings by mixing some plain yogurt with pureed canned or ripe fruit, or a spoonful of jam or jelly in a small paper cup. Add a bit of vanilla for extra sweetness, if needed.

Fudgesicles

1 package (4 ounce) regular chocolate pudding mix (or dietetic chocolate pudding mix)

3½ cups skim milk
1 egg (optional)

Prepare as for pudding. Sweeten to taste. (An egg may be added for extra nutritional value.) Freeze in molds or paper cups and insert popsicle-stick handles.

Quickie Pops

In a mold or paper cup, mix juice (apple, pineapple, orange or grape) with 1 teaspoon melted vanilla ice cream. Mix well and freeze. Add handle when partially frozen. This has the advantage of allowing you to make just one or two rather than a whole batch. Also a good way to get kids to down some orange juice, or just use up orange juice left from breakfast.

Variation: Mash or blend pitted watermelon cubes, pour into a mold and freeze to make a popsicle.

Hint: Freeze leftover juices and syrups from canned fruits in ice cube trays. These add a "perk up" to lemonade or fruit punch. Or insert a stick in the cube before freezing and use as a popsicle.

Banana Pops

Peel 3 bananas; cut in half. Push wooden stick up center of each half and freeze. Serve this way or dip in honey and roll in toasted wheat germ, nuts or granola. If you have the time and inclination, melt 6 ounces of chocolate chips (or 12 ounces for 6 bananas) plus a few tablespoons of water. Dip the frozen bananas into the chocolate and coat to cover. Twirl to remove excess. After the chocolate sets, wrap in foil and store in the freezer.

Hint: To use up the leftover chocolate, add raisins, nuts, coconut, wheat germ or what-have-you, drop by teaspoonfuls on a sheet, and cool in the refrigerator for some nutritious candy.

Do-It-Yourself Ice Cream Sandwiches

Spread softened ice cream to the edge of any appropriate cookie (graham crackers are good, but most any cookie will do). Gently press another cookie on top. Wrap individually or stack together in foil or plastic wrap and freeze.

Hint: Ice cream cones are an all-time favorite. Punch a hole in a small foil plate or cupcake paper; place around cone to catch drippings.

Ices

Base Syrup:

2 cups water
2 cups sugar

Cook on a low boil for 10 minutes or until approximately at the jelly stage on a candy thermometer. Cool. Use as a base for orange ice, grape ice or lemon ice, below.

Orange Ice

2 cups fresh orange juice
¼ cup lemon juice or juice from
    1 lemon

Grape Ice

1½ cups grape juice
⅔ cup orange juice
3 tablespoons lemon juice

Lemon Ice

¾ cup lemon juice
1 tablespoon lemon peel,
    grated
2 cups water

Pour into trays or a small mixing bowl and freeze. Watch for "mushy" stage (1 hour) then mix in the tray and refreeze. Good alone or served by the scoop in a fruit drink.

Summer Drinks

All drinks seem to disappear from the refrigerator extra-fast at this time of year. The best warm weather drinks are easy to tote and serve. Small juice cans and the disposable boxes of drinks work well. But beverages, like everything else, should be purchased with an eye towards nutrition. Yes, the real juice drinks will cost more. But colored and flavored sugar water is still only sugar water!

Natural fruit-flavored soda in cans and bottles is becoming more widely available. Though thirst-quenching, these have little nutritional value. Many include only 10 percent fruit juice. Also be wary of artificial sweeteners. Their safety continues to be under investigation. For the average, active child, an occasional sugared soda may be preferable. If you do buy sodas, avoid varieties with caffeine since children tend to be stimulated enough already.

Keeping a good supply of drinks on hand is no easy matter. Here are a few extra ideas:

Apple Juice: Try the frozen or shelf-stable concentrate. It's delicious, sugarless and economical since it can always be stretched a bit. It can also be reconstituted with sparkling soda for a change.

Flavored Milk: When jam or jelly jars are almost empty, pour in cold milk. Shake and serve as a fruit-flavored drink.

Lemonade

3 lemons, sliced
1 cup sugar
water

Put lemons and sugar in a large container (2-quart pitcher or bowl). With a large spoon, pound the lemons to release the juice. Stir. Add a batch of ice cubes and let sit awhile, then add water to fill. Mix and serve. Or try:

1 cup reconstituted lemon juice
1½ cups sugar
2 quarts water

Mix and serve.

Grape Juice: You can double any amount of grape juice from a bottle by adding an equal amount of water and for each two cups of water added, using ½ cup sugar and one to two fresh lemons. This takes away the "heaviness" from pure grape juice and gives you more for your money.

Fruit Drink: To a glass of lemonade or light carbonated drink add fresh fruit (pineapple, grapes, strawberries or other favorites) and serve with a fork or toothpick plus a straw.

Water: Keeping cold water in the refrigerator is an excellent way to encourage consumption of this inexpensive, sugar-free beverage.

Summer Picnics

Summer means picnics, whether you camp out or simply cook out. A backyard is as exciting to a child as a national campsite may be to Mom and Dad. And don't forget to use your front stoop for a picnic lunch.

You can simplify any picnic by putting your meal on a skewer! Try a cube of cheese, ham (or any cooked meat) along with pineapple chunks, cherry tomatoes and pickles on a stick and bagged. Your meal can be eaten right off the stick or slid into a hot dog bun. The same will work for dessert, whether cookies and marshmallows for toasting or just a selection of fruits.

Finger Jell-O (see page 38) is terrific picnic fare, assuming you're not going to the desert.

Don't overlook the magic of a marshmallow roast. Children under three years old will probably eat them uncooked off their stick and still think it's a nifty event. If it's a backyard cookout, let your child later invite some of his neighborhood pals over for a social event of their own.

Take Care

Beware of children running and eating from sticks at the same time, and also of sticks with sharp points and sticks from unfamiliar (and possibly poisonous) trees such as oleander!

S'Mores

large marshmallows
Hershey bars
graham crackers

The traditional recipe! Place a toasted marshmallow and 4 squares of Hershey bar between 2 graham crackers, and you've done it!

July 4th—Independence Day

This is the only major summer holiday, so add a little red-white-and blue to your table. Make or buy cupcakes with white frosting and top with several small, red birthday candles. These will simulate firecrackers when lit.

 **Fall**

Apple Cider

In a saucepan: Heat apple cider, but do not boil. Add a stick of cinnamon and a few cloves.

In a glass coffee percolator: Put whole spices, such as stick cinnamon and cloves in the percolator basket. Pour apple juice in the bottom container. Perk a few minutes until cider is spiced to your taste.

Hot Chocolate Mix

1 box (25 ounces) non-fat dry milk
1 pound instant cocoa
1 jar (6 ounces) CoffeeMate
1 cup sugar

Mix well. Store in a covered container. To make as desired, add 3 to 4 tablespoons mix to 1 cup of boiling water. Stir.

Doughnuts

Use 1 package refrigerated biscuit dough. Punch a hole in the middle of each biscuit (a bottlecap will work). Fry in 1 inch of hot oil for about 1 minute or until lightly brown on both sides. Fry the "holes" too. When cool, shake in a bag of cinnamon mixed with sugar, brown sugar or powdered sugar.

Popcorn

Children love any and all forms (although popcorn not is recommended for children under three years old). It's as much fun to make and watch as it is to eat.

TLC Peanut Butter

If you've never made your own peanut butter, now is the time to try a batch. It's a good rainy day (or any day!) activity. The challenge is to not eat more than you shell!

1 pound (or less) peanuts in
    the shell
1 to 2 tablespoons cooking oil
salt (optional)

Shell and chop peanuts until fine in a blender, one cup at a time. Add cooking oil. (Add salt only if peanuts are *not* salted-in-the-shell variety.) This makes about 1 cup of delicious peanut butter, which should be stored in the refrigerator.

You may also want to experiment with other kinds of nuts, such as almonds, cashews or walnuts.

The easy way out: Buy peanuts already shelled.

Easy Applesauce

several apples	sweetener
¼ cup water or apple juice	lemon or Fruit Fresh
cinnamon	

Take advantage of the fall harvest by making fresh applesauce. Peel, core and slice several apples. In a blender place ¼ cup water or apple juice and add apples one at a time. Blend until smooth. Pour into a saucepan and cook on low heat for 5-10 minutes. Add cinnamon and sweetener (honey or light corn syrup, for example) to taste. A dash of lemon or Fruit Fresh will retard its "darkening" action.

Spellin' Cookies

1 package gingerbread mix
⅓ cup water

With school in progress, help with the homework by making 3-letter cookie words. Mix gingerbread mix with water. Roll out on a floured surface and cut into 3-inch round cookies. Place them on a greased cookie sheet and with a knife cut the circle in thirds and push the pieces slightly apart. Bake. When cool, make 3-letter words with frosting—a single letter on each piece.

Variation: Use Cuttin' Cookie recipe, below.

Cuttin' Cookies

3 eggs, beaten	1 teaspoon vanilla flavoring
½ cup corn oil	3 cups flour
1 cup sugar	1 teaspoon baking powder

Combine all ingredients. Work on a well-floured surface. Roll out and cut into shapes with cookie cutters or a knife. (You may wish to chill the dough before rolling out.) Bake at 350° for 8-10 minutes.

Variation:

½ cup shortening	1 teaspoon vanilla
1 cup sugar	2 cups flour
1 egg	1 teaspoon baking powder
1 tablespoon milk	1 teaspoon nutmeg

Roll out on a floured surface. Cut into shapes. Bake on a greased cookie sheet at 375° for 6-8 minutes.

Hints:

- Consider using your playdough shape makers for extra fun and games! Or cut around your child's hand.

- Freeze extra cookie dough in clean frozen juice cans which are open at both ends. When ready to use, push out, slice and bake.

Edible Decorating Glue

Spread cookie with a thin coating of honey, then dip into shredded coconut, toasted wheat germ or cookie decors.

Halloween

Halloween is the holiday second only to Christmas in excitement for your child. Full understanding of Halloween comes at a surprisingly early age—costumes and candy, and not necessarily in that order.

Enjoy carving pumpkins while you can, because by the time your children are in grade school they will probably take over the responsibility—and the fun. Never carve a pumpkin more than two days before Halloween.

Better yet, decorate your pumpkins with permanent markers and use them for cooking on or after Halloween. Use a cleaned-out pumpkin for cooking and as a serving bowl for a stew.

Cooked Pumpkin

Use this method to cook pumpkin for a vegetable dish or for pumpkin cake.

Wash pumpkin; cut into large pieces. Remove the seeds and strings or fibers. Put pumpkin pieces, shell side up, in a baking pan and bake in a 325° oven for 1 hour or more, until pumpkin is very tender. (Microwave ovens can do this in less time.) Scrape pulp from the shells; put through a food mill or ricer. If the pumpkin is not thick enough to stand in peaks, simmer it in a saucepan on top of the range for 5-10 minutes, stirring constantly. Freeze in family-size servings.

Toasted Pumpkin Seeds

Don't throw away those wet, string-laden seeds from your pumpkin. They are a delicious treat! Wash the seeds and remove the strings to the best of your ability. Soak the seeds overnight in salted water (1½ teaspoons salt per ⅔ cup water). Then place the seeds in a low baking pan in the oven at 300° for approximately 20 minutes or until golden. Eat with or without removing the shells.

Of course, you can squirrel away a few seeds (not toasted) and plant them in the springtime in your garden.

Pumpkin Fries

Cut a small fresh pumpkin in half. Peel. Cut into matchsticks, and toss with 2 or 3 tablespoons peanut oil. Bake on a cookie sheet in a hot oven until brown and tender. Stir often. Sprinkle with cinnamon to taste.

Pumpkin Candy

See Fruit Roll recipe on page 42. Use canned pumpkin in place of fruit to tailor this recipe for Halloween.

Pumpkin Cup

Cut a "cap" from an orange, preferably the navel variety. Remove the inside pulp and fill with fruit or candy. Put a toothpick on the top of the "cap" which can be used as the eating utensil. Also, scratch a face on the orange and trace the "face" with a ball-point pen so the features stand out.

Pumpkin Muffins

1½ cups flour
½ cup sugar
2 teaspoons baking powder
1 teaspoon cinnamon
½ teaspoon ginger
¼ teaspoon cloves
½ cup raisins
1 egg, slightly beaten

½ cup milk
½ cup solid pack pumpkin, canned
¼ cup butter or margarine, melted
2½ teaspoons sugar mixed with ½ teaspoon cinnamon

Sift together the first six ingredients into mixing bowl. Stir in raisins. Combine egg, milk, pumpkin and melted butter. Add wet ingredients to sifted mixture, mixing only until combined. Fill greased muffin pans ⅔-full; sprinkle with cinnamon-sugar. Bake in 400° oven for 20-25 minutes. Makes a dozen muffins.

Hint: Canned pumpkin labels often carry additional recipes and cookbook offers.

Pumpkin Dessert Cake

See recipe on page 80.

Dessert Pumpkins

- To make orange frosting for cakes, cupcakes or cookies, add equal drops of red and yellow food coloring to white frosting.

- To make black frosting, mix the following together and add to white frosting:

    1½ teaspoons green food
        coloring
    1½ teaspoons red food
        coloring
    5 drops blue food coloring

- Candy corn can be used for the eyes, nose and mouth of a "face."

Thanksgiving

This warm, family holiday centers around a large turkey dinner which most children thoroughly enjoy. It's traditional to stuff a turkey, but try to avoid over-stuffing your children.

Candied Cranberries

This festive holiday snack gives the older toddler a chance to "help."

2 cups fresh firm cranberries	1 cup water
4 cups sugar	pinch of cream of tartar

Wash berries and dry on a towel. With a small skewer or heavy blunt pin, prick each berry through (or have your toddler do it). Combine 3 cups sugar, 1 cup water and cream of tartar in a 2- or 3-quart saucepan. Cook over medium heat until mixture reaches 234° (soft ball stage) on a candy thermometer. Remove from heat, pour in cranberries, and stir gently to coat each berry. Let stand at room temperature for at least 12 hours.

Then bring cranberries to a simmer over medium heat, stirring occasionally. Drain berries in a sieve over a bowl. Put syrup back on heat. Bring to a boil and boil rapidly to hard ball stage (250°). Remove from heat and dip in cranberries to coat with syrup. Lift berries out with a slotted spoon and cool on wax paper. If a pool of syrup forms around the berry, lift berry to a clean spot. When cool, roll berries a few at a time in the remaining sugar. Leftover syrup can be used on ice cream or for candied fruit.

Pumpkin Ice Cream Pie

1 quart vanilla ice cream
1 can (15 ounce) pumpkin
½ cup sugar

prepared pie shell (baked) or
    graham cracker crust
whipped cream (optional)

Soften ice cream and mix in pumpkin. Add sugar. Freeze in a prepared crust. Top with whipped cream before serving.

Pumpkin Dessert Cake

Children are seldom delighted with pumpkin pie. This recipe lets you have your traditional pumpkin dessert, but in a form your children will love.

1¼ cup oil
4 teaspoons vanilla
1 cup honey
1 cup molasses or sugar
4 eggs
2 cups pumpkin or 1 can (15
    ounce) of pumpkin
½ cup wheat germ

2 cups whole wheat flour
1½ cups white flour
2 teaspoons baking soda
2 tablespoons cinnamon
1 tablespoon nutmeg
2 teaspoons ginger
2 teaspoons ground cloves

Combine the first six ingredients and mix well. Combine dry ingredients, mix well, then combine with wet ingredients. Mix until blended. Bake at 350° in two greased bread pans for 1 hour or in a 9″ x 13″ pan for 35 minutes. Top with Cream Cheese Frosting, below.

Variation: You can also make drop cookies from this batter. Bake them at 350° for 10 minutes.

Cream Cheese Frosting

3 ounces cream cheese
6 tablespoons butter or
   margarine

1 teaspoon vanilla
1 tablespoon milk
2 cups powdered sugar

This is a good topping for the Pumpkin Dessert Cake. Mix ingredients and spread on cooled cake or cookies. Extra frosting makes an excellent filler between two graham crackers.

Apple Turkeys

Use an apple as the "body." Cut "tail feathers" from orange peels and attach with toothpicks to the apple. Cut the head and feet from heavy paper and tape to toothpick "neck" and "legs" which are then stuck into apple.

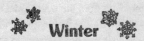

Winter

Take advantage of what is right outside your door—fresh snow! If you find some room in your freezer, pack away clean snow in a plastic bag to use come July, for snow cones or a mini-snowball fight!

Easy Ice Cream Snow

1 cup milk
1 egg, beaten

½ cup sugar
1 teaspoon vanilla

Blend the above well and add clean, fresh snow until mixture is absorbed. (May not be advisable in areas with poor air quality.)

Orange Snow: Spoon some thawed orange juice concentrate over a dish of snow.

Maple Snow: Pour maple syrup over a cup of snow.

Maple Snow Candy

Fill large pans with fresh, clean, firmly packed snow. Boil real maple syrup until it reaches the soft-ball stage, then pour it in a thin stream from a large spoon onto the snow. After the syrup has started to harden, it can be lifted in sections with a fork and twisted into elaborate shapes.

Snow Mousse

2 cups heavy cream   1½ teaspoons vanilla
1½ cups powdered sugar   large bowl of clean, fresh snow

Combine cream, sugar and vanilla. Whisk in snow gradually, adding more snow until mixture is thick and creamy. Sugar and flavorings may be added.

Christmas

Here are some decorating ideas that begin in your kitchen:

- Hang cookies on a tree by pushing a plastic straw into a hot cookie just removed from the oven. Twist out a hole at the top. Remove straw. Thread a ribbon through hole.

- String popcorn after it has been allowed to stand long enough to lose its crispness. Popcorn can also be dyed by dipping it in cranberry juice or other colored beverages.

- Tie bells on a ribbon around a bread basket to add a cheery note to your table.

Festive Ideas

- Make "wreath" pancakes and serve with strawberry syrup.

- Serve cooked peas in a scooped out tomato.

- Make a Snack Tree by covering a conical styrofoam form with green paper. With toothpicks, attach enough edibles, such as cheese cubes, cherry tomatoes, grapes, cauliflower, green pepper and carrot slices, to cover the tree. Serve with a dip.

- Use pointed paper cups for making lime gelatin "trees." Cut away paper when mold is firm and decorate with cream cheese.

- Create an Orange Sip by rolling an orange between your hands until it is soft. Use a knife to cut an "X" in the orange. Insert a porous peppermint stick in the "X" and sip away!

Christmas Trees a la Rice Krispies

You can devise many holiday treats using the well-known Rice Krispies bar recipe, including these mini-Christmas trees.

5 cups Rice Krispies	10 to 12 regular size
¼ cup margarine or butter	marshmallows
4 cups mini-marshmallows or 1	toothpicks
bag (6 to 10 ounce) regu-	green food coloring
lar marshmallows	red cinnamon candies

Melt margarine in a 3-quart saucepan; add 4 cups of marshmallows and cook over low heat. Stir constantly until syrupy. Remove from heat. Add green food coloring until mixture attains a fairly dark green color. Add cereal and stir until well-coated. With buttered hands, shape into conical forms. Cool. Stick a toothpick through a marshmallow and stick into the bottom of the "tree" to serve as the tree base. Decorate with red candies.

Variations:

- **Snowman:** Form three balls of mixture in decreasing size. Roll in coconut, stack and decorate.

- **Balls:** Shape balls of mixture around a nut or date, then roll in colored sugar.

- **Pops:** Shape pops from the mixture in an oval around a wooden popsicle stick.

- **Tarts:** Press mixture into a buttered muffin tin to form a tart shell. Fill with fresh fruit or ice cream.

- **Wreaths:** Shape mixture into a "doughnut." Decorate with red candies.

Gingerbread House

1 gingerbread mix
⅓ cup water
Frosting Cement, below
cardboard
toothpicks

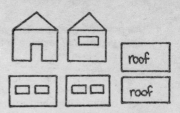

This nifty idea will delight your kids (although not necessarily the nutritionists). Fortunately, it's more to look at than eat. This simplified recipe does not take a great deal of time.

To one gingerbread mix, add ⅓ cup water. Mix well and roll out into ½-inch thickness. It will work best if you take the time to make a cardboard pattern. The base of the house will be about 4" x 6". It will stand about 3½ inches high to the eaves line. You will need six sections.

Cut the door and windows before baking, but do not remove the pieces until after baking. Extra dough can be molded into little cookie people. Bake on a greased sheet for maximum hardness, but do not allow the edges to burn (approximately 15 minutes). The house is "glued" together with Frosting Cement (see below). Use toothpicks when or where necessary. Use the Frosting Cement to hold the base to the plate so that it will stand. Let the frame dry before adding roof.

For decoration:

- **Snow Landscape:** Sprinkle coconut around house, or use cotton.

- **Roof:** Spread with icing and cover with mini-marshmallows, coconut, sprinkles, decors or candied fruit slices, halved.

- **Path:** Build with small circle candies such as M & Ms, plain chocolate candies, Lifesavers or sliced gum drops.

- **Chimney:** Pile two or three hard circle candies or sugar cubes as a chimney. Cement with frosting.

- **Trees:** Create with green gum drops, lollipops, pine cones, inverted sugar cones, or tree cookies.

- **Snowmen:** Shape two balls from leftover frosting. Let dry. Or stack large marshmallows. Attach with frosting.

Frosting Cement

2 egg whites, beaten
½ teaspoon cream of tartar
2 cups powdered sugar

A smooth, hard-drying icing. Beat 2 egg whites stiff with ½ teaspoon cream of tartar. Add 2 cups powdered sugar and beat 5 minutes with an electric mixer. Since this mixture dries quickly, keep it covered with a damp cloth when not in use.

Traditional Gingerbread Men

⅔ cup butter or margarine   1 egg
½ cup sugar   ¾ cup molasses
2 teaspoons ginger   3 cups all-purpose flour, sifted
1 teaspoon cinnamon   ½ teaspoon baking soda
½ teaspoon nutmeg   raisins

Put shortening, sugar, spices and egg in a large mixer bowl. Mix until well blended. Add molasses and mix well. Sift together flour, baking powder and soda. Stir into shortening mixture and mix well. Refrigerate at least 2 hours for easier handling.

Roll out on floured board and cut gingerbread men shapes. Use bits of raisin for eyes, nose and buttons. Sprinkle with granulated sugar, if desired. Bake on greased cookie sheets at 375° for 8-10 minutes. Makes about a dozen 5-inch gingerbread men.

Valentine's Day

Valentine's Day is a day to make good use of your heart-shaped cookie cutter—on toast, sandwiches, cheese slices, red Finger Jell-O and, of course, cookies.

Valentine Krispies

Use the Rice Krispies marshmallow bar recipe (see Christmas Trees on page 83). Add red food coloring to the syrup just before mixing it with the dry cereal. Mold in a heart-shaped, greased cookie cutter. Take it out and put on a plate to cool.

Need a heart-shaped cake pan, but have no such pan? Bake a round and a square layer cake (8-inch or 9-inch) and combine them this way:

Spring

The egg is often used symbolically as part of the Easter and Passover celebrations. It symbolizes new life in both traditions.

An Easter egg hunt—indoors or out—is always great fun. Add some hidden peanuts-in-the-shell to provide extra hunting fun. (Do keep an accurate count of eggs hidden indoors!)

Decorating Easter Eggs

Use hard-boiled eggs since they can best take the stress of handling by small children. Take advantage of food coloring in your pantry. Let your eggs soak for at least half-an-hour in bowls of hot water with different colors in each. After they are removed, let them dry and decorate them with non-toxic magic markers. It's a great medium and easy for kids to handle. An egg carton or a cardboard tube cut into sections make excellent drying and decorating stands. When finished, put a drop of shortening on your hands and rub over each egg to give it a shine and to set the color. You can also glue on additions such as ribbon, rick-rack and even plastic "eyes."

Egg-Shaped Cookies

Make an egg-shaped cookie cutter by bending and shaping the open end of a 6-ounce juice can. Decorate with a variety of icings, or with Egg Yolk Paint, below.

If you're not up to making your own dough, use a roll of refrigerated sugar cookies and shape.

Egg Yolk Paint

Blend ¼ teaspoon water with one egg yolk. Divide among several small dishes and put different food coloring into each dish. Paint designs on cookies before baking.

Jell-O Eggs

Save egg shells (either blown-out ones or half shells). Rinse and let stand at least a day. Fill with Finger Jell-O (page 38). Crack and remove shell after Jell-O has hardened. Regular Jell-O can also be used here, but use half of the cold water called for.

Egg Tree

A branch can be decorated attractively using decorated egg shells. Here you must blow out the inside of the raw egg before decorating and hanging it. Use glue to affix strings. If a budded branch is put in a narrow-necked vase with water, leaves will soon adorn the branch along with the decorated eggs.

Bunny Salad

Place a canned pear half on a bed of lettuce. Add raisins for eyes, a strawberry (with a toothpick) for the nose, toothpicks for whiskers and American cheese (or paper) for the ears.

Bunny Biscuits

Use refrigerated biscuits. Cut one in half horizontally, then cut one of those pieces in half to use as the head. Cut the remaining piece in half for the ears. Pinch out a bit for the tail and bake as directed.

Bunny Ice Cream Dish

Arrange three balls of vanilla ice cream on a plate to form a bunny. Use a large one for the body, a medium one for the head and a small one for the tail. Cover with shredded coconut. Use jelly beans or almonds for the eyes and nose, paper cutouts for the ears and toothpicks or licorice string for whiskers.

Bunny Cakes

Version One: Bake a cake in a heart-shaped pan, and cover it with white or pink frosting. Decorate it as shown in the diagram below, using paper cutouts for ears, jelly beans for eyes and nose and icing or licorice string for whiskers.

Version Two: Bake cake in one layer cake pan. Cut layer in half, as shown. Stand layers side by side, attaching them with a filling of your choice. Shape rabbit by cutting out notch to make a body and head. Use notch for tail. Frost with fluffy white frosting and sprinkle with coconut. Insert paper ears, jelly beans for eyes and nose, and licorice strings for whiskers. Sprinkle green-tinted coconut and more jelly beans on the cake platter.

Tinted Coconut: Add a few drops of food coloring to a small amount of water in a bowl; add coconut and toss with a fork until evenly distributed.

Or

In a small jar, toss 1½ cups coconut with 1 to 2 tablespoons fruit-flavored Jell-O. Shake well.

Easter Baskets

- Use a pipe cleaner as a handle on a margarine tub. Fill with seedless green grapes.

- Decorate a frosted cupcake with green-tinted coconut. Use pipe cleaners to form basket handle.

So You're Having a Birthday Party!

Here are a few ideas and insights that might help you keep birthdays the happy days they're supposed to be. Plan ahead. Keep it short and simple. And, above all, keep it moving!

The most important "rule" is one that is often the most difficult to follow:

The number of juvenile guests should not exceed the number of years in your child's age.

Keep in mind that young children enjoy most what they know best. This is not the age for surprise parties. Build on tradition—the same songs, cakes, balloons, candles, gifts and games.

For more party ideas for these ages, see Vicki Lansky's *Practical Parenting Birthday Parties* (Bantam, 1986).

Year One

This party is really for adults. At least one set of grandparents plus an aunt, a cousin, an uncle, the babysitter, a neighbor or friend will want to attend. The food can be fancy and oriented towards adults because your baby will care very little about it, unless he or she can get hands into the goo or the ice cream. Your child will be bewildered by the presents, but will truly enjoy the attention, excitement and picture-taking.

If the party also includes mothers with their small children, consider a BYOHC (bring your own high chair) party. Provide disposable bibs, Wash & Dries and teething biscuits as favors. Have film and your camera ready. There is only one first birthday party!

Limit the party to an hour.

Year Two

By the second year, the miracle of maturation gives your child a clear understanding of a birthday party, its food and its presents. Keep the party as small—yes, as small—as possible. Two-year-olds are a bit young for games yet. A supply of toys and balloons works well. Since sharing is not usually a strong point at this age, you may spend some time refereeing. Odds are you'll also be entertaining the mommies and possibly the daddies.

A good food idea for the children is something simple like cupcakes and/or ice cream cones with sprinkles. Disposable bibs and Wash & Dries may still be in order. The birthday cake with the candles may be for the adults, but only after its candles are blown out and the children are served their share. Don't waste good food on the kids—they usually don't eat more than a few bites.

Limit the party to an hour or an hour and a half.

Year Three

Now you are entering the realm of the more traditional birthday party. Games can be played and enjoyed, although they must definitely be led. Keep it simple. Three to five short games should suffice. Avoid competitive games unless everyone can get a prize. A quiet game or storytelling are a better prelude to refreshments than active games. (See list of games at the end of this chapter.)

Your three-year-old can begin to learn the social graces. Manners won't be ideal but this is a good starting point. Greeting guests, opening presents, verbalizing thanks and saying good-bye are concepts to be discussed before the party and congratulated on afterwards.

Your child should also be consulted about the guest list. He or she can help mail or deliver the invitations and help choose or frost the cake. Written thanks for presents are not necessary.

Food should again be simple. If you are dying to try an unusual form cake, don't. Children do enjoy form cakes; just don't get carried away. Three-year-olds judge most cakes by their icing alone.

Also save yourself time and hassle by scooping out ice cream balls ahead of time. Place them in a cupcake paper and store in the freezer until you're ready for them. Or buy ice cream cups and serve them with the wooden spoons.

A fun placecard is a cookie with each child's name written in icing. Or let each child decorate his or her own cookie. Provide icing, a popsicle stick and decorations such as sprinkles, nuts, raisins, chocolate chips and coconut.

Do include a "hunt" (candy, peanut or otherwise) in your party. A party hat or small plastic bag is an appropriate holder. Save some extra goodies in case any child totally misses the boat.

While candy is an integral part of any party, you may want to include some more nutritious treats. Consider these:
dietetic or carob-covered raisins
Finger Jell-O (see page 38)
Fruit Roll (see page 42)
peanuts in shells
pretzels tied with ribbons
raisins, nuts and sunflower seeds
sugarless bubblegum
Uncandy Bars (see page 39)

A favorite treat that makes a birthday special is Candy Cookies, (page 92). Bake them either for a party at home or at nursery school. Only add the candies to the cookie tops and use the Cornell Triple-Rich Formula. You will compromise the kids' love for candy with a bit of nutrition.

Limit the party to an hour and a half.

Candy Cookies

1 cup oil
1 cup brown sugar, packed
½ cup sugar
2 eggs
2 teaspoons vanilla
1½ teaspoons baking soda

2¼ cups flour (see Cornell Triple-Rich Formula, page 62)
1 cup (or less) M&Ms Plain Chocolate Candies

Cream shortening, sugars, eggs and vanilla. Mix dry ingredients and combine with creamed mixture. Drop by teaspoonfuls on an ungreased cookie sheet. Flatten to not more than 2-inch diameter. Decorate with 4 to 6 candies per cookie, but do make sure (to avoid being hassled) that the number of candies *is the same for every cookie.*

Bake at 375° for 8-10 minutes. The candies often crack after baking. This recipe makes 2-4 dozen cookies depending on the size of your teaspoonful.

We can offer no advice on presents, prizes or party favors. You alone must live with your budget and your neighbor's. But remember, *more does not mean better.*

Year Four

Most of what goes for a three-year-old's party is applicable here and more so. By now, the moms and dads are no longer on the sidelines, so it's up to mom (or whomever) to keep the ball rolling. If it's too much for you to be leader, songmistress, photographer, waitress and clean-up committee, have someone help you— possibly a neighborhood teenager.

Alleviate the awkwardness of the party's start, waiting for all the guests to arrive, by planning some activity. String a birthday necklace, decorate a favor bag, or even open the presents.

Four-year-olds anticipate games eagerly. A variety of short games is good for their short attention spans. (See list at end of chapter.) In addition to some games, a clown or puppet show would be a treat. Check the talents of some of the older children in your neighborhood.

You may find yourself holding the party around lunch or dinner. The following is a list of foods with the best chance of being eaten:

American grilled cheese sandwiches
Pizza
Macaroni and cheese
Hamburgers
Peanut butter and jelly sandwiches (cut with cookie cutter)
Potato chips (individual bags are a treat)
Carrot sticks
Dill pickles
Apple wedges
Mandarin oranges
Green grapes (seedless)
Juice (apple, pineapple, orange)
Chocolate milk

Sandwiches should be "crustless!" After all, this is a party. Avoid drinks that stain. Juice boxes are special as well as spill-proof!

Make portions small. Children often eat very little because they are too excited.

For a different ice cream treat, cut off the tops of some oranges and scoop out the inside. Put in orange sherbet and freeze until ready to serve.

Consider a Do-It-Yourself-Sundae, letting the children help themselves to their favorite ice cream toppings: fudge, honey, maple syrup, granola, nuts, crushed pineapple, coconut and whipped cream.

Or make a clown cone. Top a scoop of ice cream with a sugar cone for a hat and decorate a face on it. Reddi-Whip makes good "hair." Make ahead of time and freeze.

Do not feel you have to seat a group of children in your dining room. Any appropriate room with a vinyl tablecloth on the floor and low tables (coffee table or card tables on books or bricks) will work just fine.

While you can specify a time for the guests to be picked up, returning your guests to their homes lets you end the party on your schedule.

Limit the party to two hours.

Year Five

While home parties for this age are still recommended, away-from-home parties now begin to work for kids. Avoid movies but check out hamburger franchises, pizza parlors, ice cream parlors, gymnastics programs, skating rinks and even your local zoo.

```
Birthday Party Dangers
            Beware of:
1) Little girls with long hair blowing out candles (hair burns).
2) Children running with straws or lollipops in their mouths.
3) Children playing with (and choking on) uninflated or
   broken balloons.
```

Preschool Games

Let your birthday child be the first to be IT in a game.

Plan more games than you think you'll need in case some turn out to be too hard or unpopular. On the other hand, don't feel you must play all the games you planned—or any the birthday child doesn't like or isn't good at.

The younger the guest, the more likely that he or she may not want to play every game, so have alternatives, such as coloring books or puzzles, available.

Games are listed in progressive order for younger children, ages two to three, to older children, ages four to five.

- **Ball roll:** Sitting in a circle with legs spread, children roll a ball from one to another.

- **Tell a story:** Read from a book with large pictures or use your imagination. Keep it short.

- **Songs:** Ring-Around-the-Rosy; Farmer-in-the-Dell; London Bridge; Eensy Weensy Spider; Hokey-Pokey.

- **Animal parade.** March around as an elephant, a bunny, a dog, a cat, a bird, a kangaroo or another animal.

- **Pin the Tail on the Donkey:** Or pin the nose on the clown.

- Drop (or toss) a bean bag into a basket.

- Simple Simon (keep it simple).

- **Balloon push:** Outside it can be done with a kick, inside crawling and using one's nose.

- **Kangaroo race:** Hop, holding a balloon between the knees.

- **Ring the bell:** Hang a bell in a tree outside or a doorway inside; children throw a bean bag or Nerf ball at the bell so it will ring when hit.

- **Musical chairs:** The way you remember it or a variation. Pass a plastic or tin plate; the holder when the music stops is "out."

- **Dress up:** Have a large pile of oversized clothes, hats and shoes, that they all race to get into simultaneously (take photos).

- **Duck, Duck, Grey Duck:** A circle game of catch.

- **Doggie, Doggie, Who's Got the Bone?** Children sit in a circle; one in the center is blindfolded and an object is given to another child. Then all children put their hands behind their backs and the group recites, "Doggie, Doggie, Where's your bone? Someone has taken it far from home!" With blindfold off, the child now is given three chances to guess who has the "bone."

- **Shoe race:** Everyone removes shoes and places them in a pile. On signal they race to find and put on their own shoes (forgo buckling and tying) and race to the finish line.

- Bingo!

Kitchen Crafts

Work and play are not separate in a child's world—they are inseparable. The same goes for their relation to you—you work and they play! Your time is often spent in the kitchen and your child's will be too, so give him or her a chance to do some creative "messing around!"

The first opportunity is the kitchen itself, with all the grown-up tasks to be done. Many of these can be shared with your youngsters. Don't expect perfection; remember they are new to these tasks.

- Washing dishes, dirty or not.
- Setting the table.
- Folding napkins.
- Washing and cleaning vegetables.
- Scrubbing the floor.
- Cleaning your kitchen sink—it will be spotless.

Doughs, Clays and Pastes

Your kitchen can serve as the starting place for many fun activities. If you've never made your own modeling clay, now is the time to start. Following are three recipes, each with special characteristics. Experiment to find your favorite. (Your child's age may also determine which you'll use.)

When using any form of modeling clay, don't neglect those necessary pieces of equipment: cookie cutters, rolling pins (real or play), plastic knives, bottle caps, extra flour, uncooked spaghetti or macaroni, walnut half-shells and others, limited only by your and your child's imaginations.

No-Cook Playdough

1 cup white flour	1 teaspoon alum
½ cup salt	food coloring
2 tablespoons vegetable oil	½ cup water

Mix first four ingredients. Add food coloring to the water. Gradually add small amounts of water until mixture attains the consistency of bread dough. You may not use the entire ½ cup of water. You can make colors not commercially available, such as purple, by creatively mixing colors. Store in an airtight container or plastic bag. It lasts a long time. (If you can't find alum at the grocery store, it is available at the drugstore.)

Stove-Top Playdough

1 cup white flour	2 teaspoons vegetable food
¼ cup salt	coloring
2 tablespoons cream of tartar	1 tablespoon oil
1 cup water	

Mix flour, salt and cream of tartar in a medium pot. Add water, food coloring and oil. Cook and stir over medium heat 3-5 minutes. Mixture will look like a globby mess and you'll be sure it's not turning out, but it will. When it forms a ball in the center of the pot, turn out and knead on a lightly floured surface. Store in an air-tight container or plastic bag. Edible but not as tasty as Playdough a la Peanut Butter!

Playdough a la Peanut Butter

18 ounces peanut butter
6 tablespoons honey
cocoa or carob (optional)

non-fat dry milk or milk plus
    flour to the right
    consistency

Mix. After shaping, decorate (raisins?) and eat!

When your child is old enough to appreciate something a bit more permanent, add "real" homemade clay to your bag of tricks.

Clay for Play and Posterity

Baking Method

1 cup salt
½ cup water

2 tablespoons vegetable oil
2 cups flour

Mix salt, water and oil. Add flour. After shaping, the clay can be baked at 250° for several hours.

Overnight Drying Method

1 cup cornstarch
2 cups baking soda (1 pound)
1¼ cups cold water

food coloring, tempera or
    acrylic paints (optional)
shellac or clear nail polish
    (optional)

Mix cornstarch, baking soda and water. Stir in a saucepan over medium heat for about 4 minutes until the mixture thickens to the consistency of moist mashed potatoes. Remove from heat, turn out onto a plate and cover with a damp cloth until cool. Knead as you would bread dough. Shape as desired or store in airtight container or plastic bag.

To color, add a few drops of food coloring to the water before it is mixed with starch and soda. Or objects may be left to dry and then painted with tempera or acrylics. Dip in shellac or brush with clear nail polish to seal.

Clay Christmas Ornaments (Oven Drying Method)

4 cups flour
1 cup salt
1 teaspoon alum
1½ cups water

food coloring, poster paints,
acrylic paints or markers
clear shellac, spray plastic or
nail polish

Mix ingredients well in a large bowl. If the dough is too dry, work in another tablespoon of water with your hands. Dough can be colored by dividing it into several parts and kneading a drop or two of food coloring into each part. Roll or mold as desired. (If you can't find alum at the grocery store, it is available at the drugstore.)

To Roll: Roll dough ⅛-inch thick on lightly floured board. Cut with cookie cutters dipped in flour. Make a hole in the top, ¼-inch from the edge, with the end of a plastic straw dipped in flour. Shake the dots of clay from the straw and press on as decorations. Thread ribbon or wire through the hole to hang ornament.

To Mold: Shape dough into figures (such as flowers, fruits and animals) no more than ½-inch thick. Insert a fine wire in each for hanging.

Bake ornaments at 250° on an ungreased cookie sheet for about 30 minutes. Turn ornaments over and bake another 1½ hours until hard and dry. Remove and cool. When done, sand lightly with fine sandpaper until smooth. Paint with food coloring, plastic-based poster paint, acrylic paint or markers. Paint both sides. Allow paint to dry and seal with clear shellac, spray plastic or clear nail polish.

This recipe makes about 5 dozen 2½-inch ornaments.

Clay Cookie Ornaments (Overnight Drying Method)

2 cups salt
⅔ cup water

1 cup plus cornstarch
½ cup cold water

Mix salt with ⅔ cup water and boil. Add cornstarch and remaining water. Stir. If mixture doesn't thicken, set back on the stove. Sprinkle extra cornstarch on table and rolling pin. Roll out dough and cut with cookie cutters. Use a plastic straw to make hole at the top for hanging. Dry and decorate. Use paint, glitter and so on to decorate. These are not edible!

Bread Clay Recipe

6 slices white bread
6 tablespoons white glue

½ teaspoon detergent or 2
teaspoons glycerine
food coloring

Whoever said that plain old white bread isn't worth anything! Remove the crusts from the bread and knead bread with white glue and detergent or glycerine. Knead mixture until it becomes non-sticky. Separate into portions and tint with food coloring. Shape and when done, brush with equal parts glue and water for a smooth appearance. Let dry overnight to harden. Acrylic paints, plastic spray or clear nail polish will seal and preserve your child's art "treasures."

Homemade Silly Putty

2 parts Elmer's white Glue
1 part Sta-Flo liquid starch

Mix well. Putty must dry a bit before it is workable. It may be necessary to add a bit more glue or starch; you will have to experiment. (Recipe may not work well on a humid day.) Store in an airtight container. Homemade Silly Putty has the same nasty characteristics of commercial Silly Putty. Beware of contact with clothes and carpet. If you use Elmer's School Glue instead of regular white glue, putty doesn't bounce or pick up pictures, but it makes a gooey delight your kids will love. Use on a smooth surface.

You will probably find yourself supporting Borden's Company (makers of Elmer's) by buying both its regular glue and its more washable school glue. But home paste will work for many projects.

No-Cook Paste

a handful of flour
water
a pinch of salt

Gradually add water to flour and mix until gooey. Add salt. This recipe can also be used as a quickie finger paint by adding some food coloring and working it on heavy paper or cardboard. Also works well as a papier-mache paste.

Library Paste

1 cup flour
1 cup sugar
1 teaspoon alum

4 cups water
oil of cloves or wintergreen

Mix ingredients in a saucepan. Cook until clear and thick. Add 30 drops oil of cloves or wintergreen and store in a covered container. (If you can't find alum at the grocery store, it is available at the drugstore.)

Lightweight Glue

Egg white makes a good adhesive for constructing kites. It is strong and almost weightless.

Finger Paints

Finger painting does not occupy the attention of small children for as long as we would wish (cleaning up always seems to take longer than play time). But it's worth the effort for the discovery and fun value. Do not show your child how to use finger paints as you think they should be used—experimenting is the best part for your child. Sometimes, it is fun for him or her just to feel the cool, smooth paint and see the bright colors. A linoleum floor, covered with newspapers, is often the best painting place since it often has to be cleaned after a painting session anyway! Regarding regular water-based paint: Powdered poster paint is a good investment. It can be found in art supply or crafts stores.

#1 Finger Paints

3 tablespoons sugar
½ cup cornstarch
2 cups cold water

food coloring
pinch of detergent

Mix the sugar and cornstarch and then add the water. Cook over low heat, stirring constantly, until well blended. Divide the mixture into four or five portions and add a different food coloring to each, plus a pinch of detergent (facilitates cleanup).

#2 Finger Paints

½ cup dry laundry starch
¼ cup cold water
1 ½ cups boiling water

½ cup soap flakes
1 teaspoon glycerine
food coloring

Mix starch and cold water in a saucepan. Pour in the boiling water and cook over low heat until shiny. Remove from the heat and add soap and glycerine. Divide the portions and add different food coloring.

Soapy Finger Paints

Beat warm water into Lux or Ivory Flakes to desired consistency and add paint or food coloring.

If you don't wish to go to the trouble to mix finger paints, add a drop of food coloring to aerosol shaving soap and let your child do his or her thing on a cookie sheet.

Brushes

- Try a pastry brush if you can spare yours. These have wider handles and the stiffer brush cuts down on splatters.

- Or try cotton swabs. A different swab can be used for each color so that paint (hopefully) remains unmixed and bright.

Printing

Printing—Vegetable Style

Cut a potato, carrot or turnip in half and carve out a raised design (Mom's job). Brush poster paints over the design. Or stamp the design in an ink pad. Press firmly on paper: white tissue paper, uncoated shelf paper, ribbons or anything you have around. Let dry.

Sliced citrus fruits, apples, and even onions also make lovely prints.

Printing Utensils

While sponges, plain or cut into shapes, are the most obvious printing utensils, also try some of the following: a potato masher, wooden salad fork, extract bottle bottoms and toothbrushes.

Paper Product Paraphernalia

Here are just a few ideas for using everyday items.

Straws

To make any day special, and maybe to encourage the drinking of an unfavorite beverage, try this trick. Make a cut-out (one paper plate will provide several) in a circle or special shape. Use a hole puncher to make a hole in the top and bottom of your design. Decorate or let your child do so, then weave the straw in one hole and out the other. (If you include names on your design, these could be dandy "placecards" for a birthday party.)

Paper Plates

These can be used as: hats, puppets or a clock.

Milk Cartons

There are many things you can do with your empty milk cartons. Consider this fun idea:

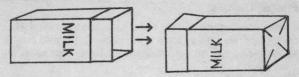

Make building blocks: Use two milk cartons of the same size. Open the top ends completely, then slide cartons together as shown to make a block. Cover with Contact paper to decorate.

Paper Cups

These can be made into:

- **Bells:** Decorate.

- **A mini-drum:** Cover top with paper and hold in place with an elastic band.

- **A telephone:** Connect two cups with a long string.

- **Spy glasses:** Attach two cups with tape, punch holes for eyes and use string to secure around the head.

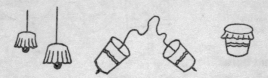

Brown Paper Bags

- Large brown paper bags make good life-size masks and costumes for young children. Help children cut out facial features and holes for the arms and let them do the rest alone.

- Brown bags can also be decorated even when they will later be used as garbage bags.

- To make a flashlight face, cut out features on the base of a bag and insert a flashlight. Twist the bag around the handle and fasten with tape, leaving an opening for the switch.

- A smaller bag makes an excellent hand puppet. (Make the "head" on the base of the bag.)

- Or make a tote bag:

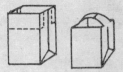

Miscellaneous Fun

Stained Glass Crayons

A good way to make use of all those broken crayon pieces (which always seem to be in over-supply) is to make stained glass crayons. Remove any covering paper and place the pieces in a well-greased muffin tin (or line each muffin section with tin foil) and put in a 400° oven for a few minutes (or until melted). Remove from the oven and cool completely before removing from tin. If you mix the crayon colors, the circles will have a lovely stained glass effect and are great fun to color with.

Peanut Butter Bird Feeder

Spread peanut butter on each "leaf" of a pine cone. Roll in a dish of bird seed. Using a piece of yarn or wire, hang it from a tree.

Bean Bags

Bean bags were more plentiful when dried beans were lower in price. Every toy chest still needs a few. Sew three sides of two fabric squares together; add beans and sew the fourth side. Or use a small child's orphaned sock or mitten as a bean bag. Sew up!

Chase the Pepper

You don't have to understand the scientific principle to be entertained by this magic trick.

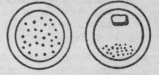

Fill a pie plate (or small sink) with water. Shake pepper on the water. Take a piece of wet soap and dip it into the water. The pepper will run away from the soap. Now shake some sugar into the clear area and the pepper will run back.

Crystal Garden

4 tablespoons salt
4 tablespoons water
4 tablespoons ammonia

4 tablespoons liquid wash
bluing

Mix ingredients. Pour over several small pieces of charcoal or pieces of sponge in a bowl. Put several drops of different-colored inks on various parts of it. Leave it undisturbed for a day. Crystals will cover it in an interesting formation, growing and spreading every day. It will be white where no ink was used. (The garden grows better in dry air than in humid air.)

How Does Your Garden Grow?

There are several easily grown items that may be of special wintertime delight for your child. He or she can do all the work.

A good functional container is a cut-down milk carton with potting soil and holes punched in the bottom for drainage. Or you may even want to use an egg-shell half. Three-quarters of an egg shell, decorated, makes a delightful pot. Better yet, the shell can be a "head" with green, growing "hair." Place "pot" in a sunny or well-lit window.

- Avocados: Though the avocado pit is a popular item to grow, it is not much fun for small children as germination is often very slow.

- **Cress:** Most types of cress are easy to grow and can even be added to salads a few weeks after planting.

- **Dried beans:** Roll a piece of paper towel and place in a clear glass. Put a bean (a lima bean, corn kernel, or other dried bean) between the paper and the side of the glass. Keep it moist. You can watch the seed send roots down and sprouts up.

- **Citrus seeds:** Place 4 or 5 seeds (orange, lemon or grapefruit) in a container and cover with ½ inch of soil. Keep soil moist by gently covering with clear wrap until the seeds have germinated.

- **Sweet potatoes:** Place a large sweet potato in a shallow dish with enough water to cover it. Keep it half-covered in water as the days pass. It will grow a lovely vine for you. If you have no luck, try a new potato since sweet potatoes are often treated to prevent growth.

- **Carrots:** Cut the green top from a carrot yourself. Place top few inches of the carrot root in water. Top will sprout again.

- **Grass seed or bird seed:** Place on a wet sponge in a shallow dish. A little water should always show above the sponge so that you know it has not dried out. Your child can "mow the lawn" if he or she can handle a scissors.

Potpourri

(Or, "I Wish I'd Thought of That!")

This final chapter is sort of a collection of everything that didn't fit anyplace else. It contains many well-used ideas passed from "practicing" parents to other new parents—practical information collected in one place for your reference.

Busy Little People Make Spots

Some tried-and-true methods for removing those spots that are sure to show up as your child grows:

- **Stamped-on prices:** Remove from plastic items with alcohol or cleaning fluid.

- **Milk spots on upholstery or carpet:** Rub in baking soda and vacuum out. Baking soda will prevent staining and keep odor away.

- **Blood stains:** Rinse in cold water. Then soak in cold water with salt before washing as usual.

- **Urine on a rug:** This requires fast action. Mix a solution of ½ cup vinegar with ¾ cup water. Apply small amounts on the stain. Give the solution a few minutes to work and then sponge from the outside to the center. Blot dry with a cloth. Keep the above solution on hand so that prompt action is possible. Another recommended solution is 1 tablespoon ammonia in ¾ cup water. Use small amounts and blot out.

- **Marks on walls and woodwork:** Wash with a solution of one cup ammonia, ¼ cup baking soda and ½ cup vinegar in a gallon of warm water. This will clean without dulling.

- **Marks on appliances and windows:** Clean without film or streaks with this solution. Mix ¼ cup alcohol, 1 tablespoon white vinegar and 1 tablespoon non-sudsy ammonia. Add enough hot water to make one quart.

With a baby:

- **Baby bottles and toys:** A few spoonfuls of baking soda in a quart of water cleans baby bottles and toys and freshens a diaper bag and plastic panties. Add baking soda to your diaper pail to prevent odor.

- **Baby's silver gifts:** To clean, rub a small amount of toothpaste over them with a damp cloth, then rinse clean.

- **After-meal mess:** After-meal "swabbing" is seldom appreciated by babies. You can ease the task by applying petroleum jelly or baby oil to your baby's chin and cheeks before a meal. Or when your little one is able, give him or her a damp wash cloth for a self-cleanup. Most (though not all) of the food will be removed and so will the hassle. You can also hold a small bowl of water on a high chair tray after a meal while your child plays with the water for a minute. Then all you need to do is wipe the clean hands dry!

With a toddler:

- **Crayon marks:** Remove from vinyl tile or linoleum with silver polish. To remove from woodwork, rub lightly with a dry, soap-filled steel wool pad.

- **Dirty white socks:** Boil in water with a slice of lemon.

- **Ballpoint ink on fabrics:** Remove by spraying hairspray directly on surface and wiping away with warm, sudsy water.

- **Bubble gum in the hair:** Peanut butter is a terrific remedy. Then you're just stuck with washing out the peanut butter. Milk chocolate and cold cream are also effective. To remove bubblegum on fabric, apply ice and scrape off as much as possible.

- **Stuffed toys:** Clean by rubbing with corn starch. Let stand briefly, then brush off.

- **Finger marks on wallpaper:** Rub chunks of soft, stale bread over wallpaper to remove.

Now You Are an M.D.—Mother-on-Duty

Motherhood, you will quickly discover, is an on-the-job paramedic training program.

First, keep in mind that feeding schedules usually disappear during illness. Even a minor illness usually means that foods give way to liquids. Give your child plenty to drink, if the child is not vomiting. Your child's appetite will make up for the lost meals when good health returns.

Your doctor may recommend a clear-liquid diet. This includes Fruit Ice, popsicles, frozen orange juice-on-a-stick, Kool-Aid, clear broth, Jell-O, fruit punches and soft drinks such as cola or ginger ale that have been allowed to go flat.

If your child won't drink the needed liquids, offer a straw when he or she is in a bathtub of clean water.

Fruit Ice is an excellent first-aid measure for cut lips and bumped mouths. It slows down bleeding and keeps swelling to a minimum, while getting your child's mind off the discomfort.

Fruit Ice

finely crushed ice
frozen juice concentrate,
    thawed

Place ice in a cup and pour juice over it. Drink or eat as a snow cone with a spoon.

First Aid Tips

- Give a child liquid medicine in a nipple, an eye-dropper or a syringe dispenser you can buy at the drugstore.

- Honey and lemon juice is a good homemade cough syrup. (Do not give to babies under one year old.)

- A small plastic hair curler makes a good "cast" for a bruised finger.

- An ice cube will help numb an area when you need to remove a splinter.

- Use a can of frozen juice or a bag of frozen vegetables as a quick, dripless compress.

- When removing a Band-Aid, rub it well first with baby oil to make it "ouchless."

- A pill is swallowed more easily in a teaspoon of applesauce.

- Treat a bee sting quickly with a paste of baking soda and water. Or use meat tenderizer and water. Ice can help numb the area.

- For diaper rash, cautiously use your hair dryer to dry a sore bottom between diaper changes. Fresh air, in any form, is the best treatment for a rampant rash. Solid vegetable shortening can be used as a diaper rash ointment.

- Immediate treatment for a burn is cold water and/or ice. For a larger burn (including sunburn), cover area with a cold, wet towel.

Illness Feeding Guideline

Sore Throat

Offer soothing suckers (such as lollipops, popsicles, orange juice-on-a-stick), ice cream and ice.

Fever

Give liquids in whatever form they will be taken. If your child won't drink large amounts, try small amounts at frequent intervals. Sometimes your child will drink more by going back to a bottle. Check with your doctor before you give aspirin or acetaminophen.

Vomiting

Forget food; wait as long as your child will let you to try small amounts of liquid. To assure a slow intake let your child suck on an ice cube or on crushed ice. Continue to add small amounts of liquids in gradually increasing intervals until you are sure your child's stomach is settled. Appropriate liquids are decarbonated sodas, sweetened tea and "Jell-O Water" (one package Jell-O to one quart of water). Wait half a day before starting easy solids such as dry crackers. If vomiting recurs, start from the top. Check with your doctor if vomiting continues into a second day.

Diarrhea

Discontinue milk (including skim, boiled or unboiled) until symptoms disappear. Serve appropriate liquids at room temperature: juices, decarbonated sodas, weak tea, "Jell-O Water" (one package to one cup tap water), and carrot soup (make by mixing one jar of commercial strained carrots with one jar of water—it replaces fluids as well as lost minerals). Easy-binding solids are: mashed potatoes, rice cereal, Jell-O, dry toast, crackers, banana and applesauce. Check with your doctor if your baby is under six months old. Give Gatorade to older children to replace lost minerals as well as fluids. Easy to remember is the BRAT diet:

BRAT Diet

Bananas	Applesauce
Rice cereal	Toast

Serve small meals from this list every four hours to control diarrhea in young children.

Constipation

Serve lots of liquids! Water, diluted prune juice, non-citrus fruit juices, fruits and yogurt are best. For very small children, add a teaspoon of dark Karo syrup to milk, formula or water. Avoid milk products, apples, bananas, rice or gelatin as they are binding.

Many well-meaning parents think their child is "constipated" because he or she has a bowel movement "only" every other day or every three days. But what is important is the child's individual, established pattern of bowel movements (or stools) and the ease of passing them. A normal frequency of stools can vary from several times a day to as infrequently as once a week, if there is no straining or discomfort. Small, very hard, dry, rock-like stools passed daily, or very large, firm, bulky stools passed once a week—and which clog up the toilet—are both signs of constipation.

Back to Eating

Here are some ideas for coaxing an ailing child back to eating when his or her health returns.

- Offer snacks frequently to break boredom, supplement small appetites and increase intake of fluids.

- Allow an "eat-where-you-want" policy.

- Try novelty eating utensils such as toothpicks.

- Serve foods in tiny portions in muffin tins or egg cartons.

- Place fruit juice in an insulated pitcher at bedside.

- Put soup in a mug.

- Make sandwich faces and cookie cutter sandwiches.

- Stage an indoor picnic on the floor.

Poisons— A Very Real Danger

Do you know the phone number of your poison control center?

> My poison control phone number is _____
> The information needed via phone or at the hospital is the child's *age, weight, type and amount of poison and symptoms*.
> Take the container with you to the phone and/or the hospital.

Poisons pose a very real danger to your child. **Write your poison control phone number down now—not later.** Later may be too late. Call this number now to ask about "Mr. Yuk" stickers. The stickers can be affixed to household containers holding potential poisons.

113

The hand of the toddler *can* be quicker than the eye. Prevention is the best and the only cure. Do not store "poisons" in low storage areas and remember that high, safe places are no longer safe when your child can climb. Lock up all your medicines. By doing so, you will convey the attitude of precaution. Poisons include household cleaners, paints, lotions, creams, polish, bleach, but especially *aspirin*! Don't get in the habit of treating medicine like candy, because it just might be eaten that way when you're not near.

Some plants are also poisonous. These include hyacinth and daffodil bulbs, dieffenbachia (all parts), caster bean (all parts), lily-of-the-valley (leaves and flowers), iris (rhizome), rhubarb (leaves, cooked or raw), wild cherries, jack-in-the-pulpit (all parts), and others. Acorns consumed in quantity can be poisonous; don't let your child chew on them.

Different poisons require different antidotes. *Before doing anything, call your poison control center.* In general, do not induce vomiting if the swallowed substance is a corrosive or petroleum product and the child is unconscious. Try to have the child drink water. If the poison is a non-corrosive substance and if the child is conscious and not convulsing, give him or her a drink of water and then try to induce vomiting. Before you follow through on these suggestions, get medical advice. *But remember to call your poison control center first.*

Always keep syrup of ipecac on hand—a safe drug for inducing vomiting. But it should not be used without advice from a poison control center, a hospital or a doctor. It is inexpensive and available at all pharmacies without a prescription. If you already have this substance in your medicine cabinet, check the expiration date on the bottle.

Choking

If your child begins to choke and he or she can breathe (as indicated by coughing or speaking), *do not do anything.*

If the air passageway is indeed blocked, then three back blows properly administered can be effective but the Heimlich maneuver has been shown to be the most effective treatment for airway obstruction in children.

To administer the Heimlich maneuver properly and know how to do it for children of different ages, take a local CPR course. It is important to administer it correctly and yet gently enough not to cause internal injuries to a child. Don't practice this at home on your children.

Traveling Tips—Eating Enroute

- As a general rule, bring along edibles that are easy on the tummy, such as crackers, cheese, fresh fruit, juices and toast with peanut butter.

- Don't forget a packet of moistened wipes or a damp wash-cloth in a plastic bag.

- Unless you have a cooler with you, throw leftovers away.

- Water varies greatly around the country and can cause problems for a baby A plastic jug of sterile water will assure you of uniformity and sterility.

- For the older baby on fresh milk, thorough cleaning of bottles and nipples is all that's required since germs cannot multiply on clean, dry surfaces. Fresh milk can be purchased everywhere, but do be sure that the container is sealed and states that is has been pasteurized.

- Or if you prefer, put pre-measured non-fat dry milk in a bottle. Add water as needed.

- If you're eating out along the way, it's wise to arrive at a restaurant before the crowd. This will usually give you the extra service you need.

- When traveling by plane, let your baby drink from a bottle during takeoffs and landings. This will relieve the pressure in the ears of a child too young to understand the technique of swallowing. An older child can suck on a lollipop or chew gum.

- A covered cake pan holds paper, pens and crayons for car traveling entertainment.

- A wide-mouth steel thermos will keep baby's bottle warm.

Some Final Pass-Along Ideas

- When your child becomes an "artist," use kitchen magnets to affix the pictures to your refrigerator instead of tape.

- In the winter, bring a dishpan full of snow inside for your child to play with.

- Recycle baby food jars. Use in your tool box; for rock collections; for freezing small quantities of food; in a muffin tin to hold paints without spilling; as a small bank; as spice jars; as decorated party favors filled with treats.

- A collection of baby food jar tops in a plastic container are a great treat for an eight-month-old.

- When your child reaches the age when he or she doesn't want foods "touching" on a dinner plate, try compartmentalized plates.

- Non-skid appliques or strips made for the bathtub are ideal for the highchair to keep baby from sliding down in the seat.

- If you can spare a bottom drawer in the kitchen, turn it into a toy drawer. It is handy both for cleanups and for fast distraction!

- If your child objects to a bib, a colorful bandana scarf will serve as one for your "cowboy" or "cowgirl."

- Do you have a baby bottle warmer? It's ideal for melting such ingredients as chocolate or shortening.

- The outgrown baby cup (with the spout) makes a good gravy container and server.

- Seal lower cupboards against busy fingers with Scotch Strapping Tape. It takes just a short strip to do the trick.

And *finally*, some food for thought from an anonymous author:

How To Bake a Cake

Light oven. Get out bowl, spoons and ingredients. Grease pan. Crack nuts. Remove 18 blocks and 7 toy autos from kitchen table. Measure 2 cups of flour. Remove Kelly's hands from flour. Wash flour off. Measure one more cup of flour to replace flour on floor. Put flour, baking powder and salt in a sifter. Get dustpan to brush up pieces of bowl Kelly knocked to floor. Get another bowl. Answer phone. Return. Take out greased pan. Remove pinch of salt from pan. Look for Kelly. Get another pan and grease it. Answer phone. Return to kitchen and find Kelly. Remove grimy hands from bowl. Wash off shortening. Take greased pan and find 1/4 inch of nutshells in it. Head for Kelly who flees, knocking bowl off table. Wash kitchen floor, wash table, wash walls, wash dishes, wash Kelly.

Call bakery.

Lie down.

INDEX

FOOD EQUIVALENTS FOR MILK

1 cup buttermilk	=	1 cup milk
1 cup yogurt	=	1 cup milk
½ cup ice cream	=	¼ cup milk
½ cup ice milk	=	⅓ cup milk
1 cup baked custard	=	1 cup milk
1 ounce (slice) Swiss cheese	=	1 cup milk
1 slice American processed cheese	=	½ cup milk
1 inch cube cheddar cheese	=	½ cup milk
1 cup cottage cheese (creamed)	=	⅓ cup milk
2 tablespoons cream cheese	=	1 tablespoon milk

MILK SUBSTITUTES

Baking and run out of milk or cream? Remember that:

If the recipe calls for:	You can substitute:
1 cup coffee cream	3 tablespoons butter plus ⅞ cup milk
1 cup heavy cream	⅓ cup butter plus ¾ cup milk
1 cup whole milk	1 cup reconstituted non-fat dry milk plus 2½ teaspoons butter or margarine or ½ cup evaporated milk plus ½ cup water
1 cup buttermilk or juice	1 tablespoon vinegar or lemon juice plus enough sweet milk to make 1 cup (let stand 5 minutes before using)

TO USE HONEY INSTEAD OF SUGAR WHEN BAKING

- Use ⅔ cup of honey for each cup of sugar called for.
- For each cup of honey that you use, deduct about 3 tablespoons of liquid for the recipe. (This does not apply to yeast bread.) In baked goods — add ½ teaspoon soda for every cup substituted.
- Reduce oven temperature by about 25 degrees and bake a little longer as honey tends to make baked goods brown faster.

To use honey instead of brown sugar, use some molasses with the honey.

SIZE OF CAN

8 ounces	=	1 cup
9 ounces	=	No. 1 flat or 1 cup
16 ounces	=	No. 1 tall or 2 cups
16 ounces	=	No. 303
12 ounces	=	No. 2 vacuum or 1¾ cups
20 ounces (18 fluid)	=	No. 2 or 2½ cups
28 ounces	=	No. 2½ or 3½ cups
46 ounces	=	No. 3 cylinder or 5¾ cups
6 lbs. 10 ounces	=	No. 10 or 13 cups

MEASURE FOR MEASURE

1 pound flour	=	4 cups
1 stick or		
¼ pound butter	=	½ cup
1 square chocolate	=	1 ounce
14 squares graham crackers	=	1 cup fine crumbs
1½ slices bread	=	1 cup soft crumbs
4 ounces macaroni		
(1–1¼ cups)	=	2¼ cups cooked
4 ounces noodles		
(1¼–2 cups)	=	2 cups cooked
1 cup long grain rice	=	3–4 cups cooked
juice of one lemon	=	3 tablespoons
grated peel of 1 lemon	=	1 teaspoon
juice of one orange	=	½ cup
grated peel of 1 orange	=	2 teaspoons
1 medium apple, chopped	=	1 cup
1 medium banana, mashed	=	⅓ cup
1 pound American cheese		
(shredded)	=	4 cups
1 pound raisins	=	3½ cups
1 pound carrots	=	4 medium or 6 small
		3 cups shredded
		2½ cups diced
1 cup milk	=	½ cup evaporated milk
		plus ½ cup water OR
		⅓ cup dry milk plus one cup water
1 cup sour milk	=	1 teaspoon vinegar or
		lemon juice plus fresh
		milk to make 1 cup (let
		stand 5 minutes before using)

WEIGHTS AND MEASURES

3 teaspoons	=	1 tablespoon
4 tablespoons	=	¼ cup
8 tablespoons	=	½ cup
16 tablespoons	=	1 cup
1 cup	=	8 ounces
1 cup	=	½ pint
2 cups	=	1 pint
2 pints	=	1 quart
4 cups	=	1 quart
4 quarts	=	1 gallon